MAVERICKS

—Ten Uncorralled Westerners

by

Dale L. Walker

Golden West Publishers

Cover designs by Bruce R. Fischer/The Art Studio

Front cover: In a Cañon of the Coeur d'Alene, by Frederic Remington, appearing in *Ranch Life and the Hunting Trail* by Theodore Roosevelt, 1902.

Back cover: Frank Luke, Jr., with his Battered Spad 13 (Photo from author's files)

Library of Congress Cataloging-in-Publication Data

Walker, Dale L.
Mavericks: ten uncorralled Westerners / by Dale L. Walker.

Includes bibliographical references.
1. Southwest, New—Biography. 2. Dissenters—Southwest, New—Biography. I. Title.
CT260.5.W35 1989 920.079—dc20 89-23338 CIP
ISBN 0-914846-42-6

Printed in the United States of America

Golden West Publishers (602) 265-4392
4113 N. Longview Ave.
Phoenix, AZ 85014, USA

Dedication

To Alice McCord Walker
with love.

Acknowledgements

All of the stories in *Mavericks* have been revised and updated from their original publication, as follows:

John Doyle Lee & the Death of the Fancher Train
(from *Real West*, January 1980)

James A. Harden-Hickey: King James I of Trinidad
(from *Frontier Times*, March 1971)

William Cowper Brann: The Iconoclast
(from *The West*, June 1970)

'Pecos Bill' Shafter & the War Correspondents
(from *By Valor and Arms*, June 1978)

John Reed: Revolutionary in Mexico
(from *El Paso Times*, January 11, 1982)

Ambrose Bierce: The Devil's Lexicographer
(from *American West*, November 1973)

Tracy Richardson: Machine-gun for Hire
(from *Soldier of Fortune*, April 1980)

Frank Luke: Arizona Balloon-Buster
(from *Aviation Quarterly*, 1978)

Robert E. Howard: Conan in the Postoaks
(from *Western American Literature*, February 1977)

Max Brand: Lorenzo of the Pulps
(from *The Retired Officer*, February 1983)

Contents

Foreword

"This is a free country," we say, but we know that freedom is relative. We know also that as the population grows and we have to live under more and tighter restrictions, it sometimes seems that we have no liberty at all. We have written freedom of speech and of religion into the Constitution but new laws go on the books every year and there is no longer a western frontier for an escape hatch. As a result, Walter Mitty fantasizes about adventures he will never have and could not survive if he had them while his grandchildren watch Rambo slaughter his enemies. We face danger and death and say, in effect, "Full speed ahead, and damn the torpedoes!"

Mavericks, by any name, exist in any age or environment. Homer's heroes are succeeded in our time by soldiers of fortune like Tracy Richardson and by military heroes like Frank Luke. Sampson, who in one day slew a thousand men with the jawbone of an ass, retains his title as champion executioner, but John D. Lee at Mountain Meadows set some sort of record of his own. We do not always admire these exceptional people, but they do capture our attention, and they always will.

If the stuff of legend is lacking, we create our own heroes from whatever raw material we have. Pancho Villa doubles for Robin Hood. If no Beowulf appears on the scene, we do what we can with Wyatt Earp. We live in a time when heroes are said to be scarce or nonexistent, but Walker's mavericks come close to filling the gap. They take matters into their own hands and suffer the consequences.

Popular biographers and historians give us plenty of true-life stories to satisfy our needs, but occasionally a particularly talented and tormented individual comes along who escapes into his own imagination. Robert E. Howard of Cross Plains, Texas, is an example. Paranoid, mother-fixated and suicidal, he eventually blew his own brains out, but before he died he created Conan the Barbarian. Since then thousands of readers have been able for a few hours to leave their own humdrum Cross Plains environment and enter the wild world of the barbarians who preceded civilization in Europe.

These ten mavericks are remarkably varied but they are all

exceptional, and they appeal to the rebel—perhaps to the barbarian—in all of us. Walker has felt their attraction and conveys it to the reader. He writes crisply and organizes well, and his pages are full of human interest. Anyone who picks up his book will find it hard to put down.

C. L. Sonnichsen
Tucson, Arizona

Introduction

If they just went straight they might go far;
They are strong and brave and true;
But they're always tired of the things that are,
And they want the strange and new.

The Yukon poet Robert W. Service called them "The Men That Don't Fit In," a longer and more poetic version of "square pegs," but he was writing, as I like to write, of people who, whether by accident or design, were different in some crucial way.

In the West, we like the word "maverick" for these people. The word is drawn from the surname of South Carolinian Samuel A. Maverick (1803-1870) who came to Texas in 1835, became a signer of the Texas Declaration of Independence, and farmed and ranched near Decrows Point in Matagorda County on the Gulf Coast. According to several accounts, Maverick took 400 head of cattle in payment for a $1,200 debt and, not being particularly interested in the cattle business, turned the animals over to somebody else who was supposed to brand them. The cattle were neglected and soon every stray and unbranded animal was known to be "one of Maverick's," and eventually any unbranded calf, cow or steer became a "maverick."

The word was too good for such limited definition and over the years grew to include human strays—dissenters, loners, independent thinkers, people who refused to be corralled or branded or owned by anybody or any doctrine, philosophy or code of conduct, no matter how prevailing.

The ten men presented here were certainly mavericks—an important factor for me in searching for subjects to write about. I am drawn to historical characters who didn't fit in, who bucked the system in some way (as did Brann and Reed), who accomplished—or at least tried to—things no ordinary person would attempt (as did Tracy Richardson and Max Brand), who had a *passion* for something (as did John D. Lee), no matter how deadly, harebrained or wrong-headed, or whose character was, at least, out-of-the-ordinary if not downright bizarre (as were Harden-Hickey's, Shafter's, Bierce's, Howard's and Luke's).

Three of these mavericks were professional warriors, five were writers, one was a pioneer and a religious zealot, and one was a confidence man and, by any standard, a mental case.

Here, among these ten men are the engineer of one of the most horrendous massacres in the history of the Territorial West; the commander of the American forces in Cuba in the Spanish-American war; a fighter in banana-republic wars and in the Mexican Revolution; an "ace" and hero of World War I; a man who is one of but two Americans buried in the Kremlin Wall; the creator of *Destry Rides Again* and Dr. Kildare; the creator of *Conan the Barbarian*; two of America's most vituperative journalists; and the man who wrote the book on euthanasia and tried to be a king.

Two of these men committed suicide; two died in battle (one of them as a war correspondent); one was executed by firing squad; one was shot in the back, "right where the suspenders cross" on the main street of Waco, Texas; one disappeared into Mexico and was never seen again; one died young, of typhus, in Russia; one ended a fabulous and far-flung career selling pots and pans door-to-door; and only two of the ten died old and in bed.

Although it happens that all ten of these characters were men, the history of the American West is filled with mavericks of the two-legged species, both male and female.

They wrote some of the most colorful pages in that history.

Dale L. Walker
El Paso, Texas

John Doyle Lee

and the Death of the Fancher Train

At first glance at least, 1857 was not an auspicious year for America: it was rather more a time we might puzzle over than conjure with. To be sure, the Dred Scott decision of the U.S. Supreme Court was handed down; a man named J. S. Pierpont composed "Jingle Bells"; the *Atlantic Monthly* and *Harper's Weekly* were launched; and Nathaniel Currier and James Ives entered partnership as print publishers. But it was the year after James Buchanan became President, and the year before the Lincoln-Douglas debates in Illinois, and four years before the great sundering of the Union that for Americans would overshadow all historic events, great and small.

Yet 1857 has a dark distinction. It was the year in which an act of consummate evil occurred, an act of such cynical mercilessness that its history still produces a shudder even 132 years distant in time and countless acts of savagery distant in human experience.

The Mormon Church, more properly the Church of Jesus Christ of Latter-day Saints, had a history of but 27 years' duration when the Fancher train entered Utah, the church having been founded in Palmyra, New York, in 1830, under the mesmerizing leadership of the Prophet, Joseph Smith.

From the beginning, Smith's flock made its progress over great, often cruel, obstacles. To outsiders in those early days, most Mormons were clannish, self-righteous, dogmatic and fanatic. To those within, most "Gentiles"—non-Mormons—were ignorant, intolerant, blaspheming infidels. And a part of this mutual paranoia was the outsider's view that the "Saints" (as the Mormons called themselves, to the fury of their enemies) often placed themselves above, or at least outside, the law.

The principal example of this was the so-called doctrine of plural marriage, formally announced by the church in 1852 but long a secret practice. Polygamy, a ruinous practice for the church, only served to deepen hatred and distrust of Mormonism, subject its members to ridicule and tighten the isolation of the church from the outside world. Polygamy made the Saints lawbreakers and renegades, yet these were roles they seemed willing to accept.

In the pre-Utah period of the church, when its headquarters were at Nauvoo, Illinois, one becomes aware of the sullen presence of a man named John Doyle Lee, a Mormon zealot born in 1812 in Kaskaskia, Illinois; a veteran of the Black Hawk War of 1832, a grey-eyed Joseph Smith chauvinist and one of the Prophet's bodyguards. Lee, together with William Hickman and Orrin Porter Rockwell, were soon to become the best-known and most feared members of the Mormon secret society known as the Sons of Dan or "Danites," an organization of thugs whose existence is undoubtable, though denied by the church. These "Avenging Angels" (another of their sobriquets) sought out enemies of the church, punishing apostates and miscellaneous other offenders in various ways, including murder.

More than any other, the act which solidified the Mormon hatred of the Gentile in the first decades of the church and whetted their thirst for vengeance, occurred on June 27, 1844. On this date, a mob attacked the jail in Carthage, Ill., not far from Nauvoo, where Joseph Smith and his brother Hyrum were incarcerated. Both were killed and the leadership of the growing sect devolved upon Brigham Young, the 43-year-old Vermont-born president of the church's Quorum of the Twelve Apostles.

By the summer of 1847, Young and his followers had made their exodus, with great travail, from Illinois and Missouri and, using maps and accounts of the western explorations of John C. Fremont, had settled in the valley of the Great Salt Lake. There, with the pioneering industry and selflessness for which they were justly renowned, the Mormons established a thriving settlement and, for a time, seemed to have found their Zion—the peace, isolation and sanctuary they had long sought.

The tranquility was short-lived. Argonauts en route to California goldfields in 1849 and other emigrants arrived and formed a growing, permanent non-Mormon population while Young (appointed governor of the Territory by President Fillmore in 1850) began a number of programs to insure Mormon dominance in Utah and to discourage settlement by outsiders. Ultimately, Young's theocratic rule, revelations of unlawful polygamous practices, and continued strife with the Gentile populace, brought conflict with the federal government. President Buchanan was urged to remove Young as governor and to authorize a military expedition to quell what was considered open rebellion.

Utah Territory had become a powder keg. Brigham Young's governorship was coming to an end, an invading army marched from the east, the church was the subject of grotesque slander and ridicule in the national press, hostile elements were everywhere. And to make matters even more incendiary, news arrived of the murder in Arkansas of a beloved churchman, the Apostle Parley P. Pratt.

Into this flammable atmosphere, with perverse timing, rolled the Fancher wagon train.

Alexander Fancher, a Tennesseean about 50 years of age, may have led previous wagon trains to California and thus had earned the title by which he was known—"Captain." He had farmed in Illinois and Missouri and married Eliza Ingram in about 1838. They were parents of eight children, ranging in age from Hampton, 19 to Christopher Carson Fancher, naturally called "Kit," age five.

Capt. Fancher had crossed the country in 1855 and in southern California had selected and bought a piece of land. He returned to Arkansas the following year to begin recruiting the families he would lead to the San Bernardino area. His original party consisted of about 65 people—11 families in 11 wagons—but he counted on picking up more as the train moved west. In addition to the Fanchers, the prosperous rural families, most of them from the northwest portion of Arkansas, which made up the train included such names as Baker, Huff, Beller, Mitchell, Prewitt, McIntyre, Dunlap, Wood, Wilson, Jones, Tackett, Eaton, Edwards, Miller, Scott and Hamilton. There were a number of pregnant women making the trek and a number of mothers nursing new-born infants.

The Fancher train, by the time it arrived in Utah Territory at least, had considerable wealth. There were some 600-900 head of cattle, oxen to pull the wagons, 20-30 horses and mules and, according to several sources, as much as $4,000 in gold among the families, together with their valuable household belongings.

The train began its move westward on March 29, 1857, the route from the Platte River via the Oregon Trail in the vicinity of Ft. Kearney, Nebraska Territory, west along the north Platte to Ft. Laramie, thence across the Great Divide to Ft. Bridger and Salt Lake City. Mindful of the fate of the Donner Party in 1846, a southern route to San Bernardino had been planned.

Capt. Fancher knew that two-thirds of the journey would be occupied in traveling to the Salt Lake and that Utah Territory was controlled by the Mormons. But he also knew that Salt Lake City lay directly on the main trails to either northern or southern California. Chances are he had little knowledge of the true extent of the turbulence into which he would lead his people.

The journey to the Salt Lake was accomplished with little difficulty and in August 1857, just over 10 years after the first party of Saints had viewed their long-sought Zion, the Fancher train, swollen now to some 140 people, including 50 children, arrived on the outskirts of the Mormon capital.

It became immediately evident to the emigrants that they would have problems. The air was electric with suspicion of all intruders and Mormon merchants were selling no provisions to outsiders. There were threats openly expressed, and rumors flew to the corners of the Territory that the Fancher party included a number of Missouri "pukes" who had participated in the murders of Joseph and Hyrum Smith at Carthage, and that certain members of the train were bragging about their complicity in the killing of Parley Pratt in Arkansas.

These and other tales continued to circulate as the Fancher train, on August 5, departed Salt Lake City south toward Iron County and the route to San Bernardino. The emigrants now were accused of poisoning a spring near Fillmore which killed some cattle, several Indians and even one white man. Stories circulated that the ox-drivers were calling their animals "Brigham," and "Joe Smith," that the Missourians with the train were harassing the normally quiescent Indian tribes of the area, and that there was much shouting and abuse as the train passed through the Mormon settlements.

How much of this is true will never be known. Certainly some of the charges were counterfeit, concocted by Mormon apologists to aid in explaining the unexplainable tragedy that was about to ensue. Some of the stories were doubtlessly true: a large number of Missourians had attached to the train and perhaps did talk loosely, and there can be little doubt that conflicts were generated by both sides.

The Fancher party made its way slowly south and in the first week of September entered the narrow strip of grassland on the rim of the Great Basin, some 320 miles south of Salt Lake City, known as the Mountain Meadows.

John D. Lee lived a short distance from the Meadows at Harmony. After farming a few years near Salt Lake, he moved in

1851 to the sparsely-populated southern Territory where he had been appointed the church's farmer-agent to the Indians. The veteran Danite, forever the unquestioning loyalist, did his work well. The tribes of the southern settlements were docile, and Lee had little problem earning their trust and keeping them in check.

Why John D. Lee, together with over 50 whites and 200 Piute and other braves joined forces against the emigrant train has never been adequately explained. Anti-Mormon writers maintain Lee merely followed orders from high levels of his church—orders perhaps even known by Brigham Young himself. Other writers theorize that Lee and his equally zealous white cohorts, forced the Indians to help in the affair and that it was perpetrated out of simple hatred for the Gentiles (and perhaps a lust for their stock and money) and with no knowledge, least of all sanction, by the church hierarchy.

A recent explanation, given in a reference work on the American West, is that the Indian tribes themselves initiated the plan, blackmailing the Mormons of the region to aid them or risk attack on their own settlements. According to this theory, the Mormons decided it would be better to join the Indians against the emigrants than to chance Indian attacks on their villages at a time when invasion by federal troops was imminent.

In any event, it appears that Lee and a handful of local Saints, on about September 6, led about 200 braves to the vicinity of the Meadows and early the next morning daubed themselves with paint, donned feather headdresses, and pushed forward toward the emigrant camp in Mountain Meadows. Some of Lee's white force had serious misgivings about what they were to do and prayed, asking God's guidance.

Still under the cover of darkness, Lee's party halted off the main trail, a mile or so south of the Fancher camp and the nearby sunken spring, only source of water for the emigrants. A sortie was made in which much of the train's livestock was run off and herded into a corral several miles distant. This was done, according to Lee, without causing an alarm; indeed, without disturbing the sleeping camp.

The emigrants rose at dawn, rebuilt their campfires and began heating coffee and cooking the morning meal. Capt. Fancher had issued orders that they would move on as soon as the camp could be cleared.

A rifle shot in the distance, followed by a volley aimed directly

John Doyle Lee

into their midst, transformed the Fancher camp into a place of wild confusion and panic. Several people fell, dead or wounded from the deadly enfilade, and there was a scurrying for cover, shouted orders, screaming women and children, a spanging of bullets striking metal, and return fire from those with weapons near at hand.

In a few minutes, when the first shock of the "Indian attack" had been supplanted by the urgency for survival, defenses were hastily organized. Capt. Fancher led a number of armed men to some rocky outcroppings near the camp, there to lay down a concerted answering fire. Wagons were dragged into a compact circle, the tongues toward the center, and pits were dug in the soft earth beneath the wheels to lower the wagons closer to the ground. Trenches were begun around the camp to impede any attack across the open ground.

In the first few minutes of firing, six or seven of the emigrant men were killed outright, several others were wounded and carried to cover where they could be tended by the women. The return fire also did some damage. Lee later wrote that a number of braves were killed and many wounded. So devastating was the return fire, in fact, that Lee claimed to have sent off couriers to Cedar City, 25 miles to the northeast, for reinforcements among the local Mormon militia.

A stalemate now established, the Fancher party took stock of their situation and found it grave. The camp had been established some 35-40 yards from the only available water supply, a sunken spring surrounded by marshy ground that would have bogged down the wagons. The attack had commenced before the morning water supply had been fetched from the spring, and as the sun rose that morning of September 7, the emigrants' plight seemed desperate. Every attempt to reach the spring drew sharp and sustained fire from the attackers.

The day drew on. Lee's requested reinforcements were riding to the Meadows from several settlements in Iron County and scouts fanned out to the north and southwest, anticipating that some of the emigrants would attempt to escape their camp to seek help either at Cedar City or along the California boundary.

Ironically, within the Fancher camp there was hope of succor—from the Mormons—since it was believed the attacking force was made up wholly of hostile Indians. But meantime, the water supply dwindled to but a few cups and desperate attempts were made to dig a well within the camp confines, an effort that failed. Emigrant leaders now decided to send three men through the attackers' lines toward Cedar City for help. One of the volunteers, a young man named William Aiden, had joined the train at Provo and had some previous association with the Saints. He felt he could secure their aid.

Aiden and his companions left the camp afoot on the night of September 9, leading their horses several miles before feeling safe enough to ride. The three men traveled nearly 15 miles from the Meadows before stopping to water their horses at a small creek. There they were ambushed, Aiden killed and the other two men wounded but escaping on foot through the brush. They were later murdered by Indian members of Lee's party.

These events were unknown in the Fancher camp and with no news of Aiden, a second volunteer party of three men slipped from the Meadows on the night of the 10th, heading for the Beaver Mountain vicinity of the California border.

Nearly all of what is known of the climax of the tragedy enacted at Mountain Meadows on September 11, 1857, derives from the testimony of John D. Lee, and in his account the reinforcements from Parowan, Harmony and other Mormon settlements arrived in the early evening of the 10th. The number of Saints now involved, Lee claimed, was over 50 and the remainder of the evening passed in completing a plan to end the stalemate and bring the emigrants out of their fortified camp. By now, too, there was unanimity in the decision that there must be no survivors among the Fancher party who could tell the tale.

On the morning of the 11th, Lee exchanged his Indian garb for his ordinary work clothes and washed the paint from his face. With a militiaman named William Bateman, who carried a white flag of truce, Lee descended from the cover of a copse of trees and walked toward the Fancher camp.

The sight of the two white men must have provided a great sense of relief to the weary emigrants, for Lee and Bateman were quickly permitted to enter the camp. Once inside, Lee lost no time and began "earnest negotiations" with Capt. Fancher and the other camp leaders. He introduced himself as the Mormon agent to the Indians and said the attack on their train had come to his attention at Harmony and that he and several other Saints in the area had sped to the Meadows, calmed the attacking tribes and now had persuaded them to a truce. He appreciated their distress, Lee told the emigrants, and knew of their water shortage, but he could not help them further unless they surrendered their arms to him and his companions. He suggested the emigrants participate in a "ceremonial surrender" to placate the warriors surrounding the camp, and promised the Fancher party safe, escorted passage to Cedar City where they could reorganize and proceed on their journey.

The emigrant leaders had little choice but to put their faith in this sincere-sounding Saint. The wounded lay in agony in their bloody dressings, the precious water supply was nearly dry, ammunition could not last much longer, there were women and children to think of, the camp was surrounded by a superior force. What else could be done than to trust the Mormon deliverers?

At about noon on the 11th, therefore, the stipulations were agreed to, the emigrants opened their camp and placed their arms and ammunition in a designated wagon together with 18 of their children, all under the age of 10. Another wagon carried the wounded—two men, one woman and perhaps one or two children. A Saint named Samuel McMurdy drove the first, another named Samuel Knight drove the second and Lee walked between the two wagons as the procession set out along the trail to Cedar City.

Behind the lead wagons about a quarter-mile, the women and older children walked; a half-mile behind these came the emigrant men, beside each of which walked an armed Mormon "guard."

A half-mile ahead of the ammunition and wounded wagons, the 200 or so Indian braves lay concealed behind the roadside brush.

The lead wagons now creaked past the Indians' position. It was at this instant that a signal was given. (According to some sources, the signal came from Major John Higbee, a Cedar City Saint, who is said to have raised his arm and shouted "Do your duty!") All that happened was quickly done, but that was the only mercy. Each Saint along the road raised his rifle and at point-blank range shot the emigrant closest to him. This initial barrage killed most of the Fancher party men, but those who ran down the road were shot, clubbed to death with rifle butts or stabbed. The melee among the men occurred simultaneously with the Indian attack ahead along the trail. All the women and their children following well behind the wagons, were hacked to death or brained with warclubs.

In the first wagon, the surviving children huddled together, paralyzed with fear at the shots and shrieks they heard coming from behind them on the trail. A stray bullet entered the wagon and shattered the elbow of three-year-old Louisa Dunlap, spattering the children with blood. The horses pulling the two wagons reared and pitched, adding to the hysteria.

There is varied testimony as to John D. Lee's active participation in this slaughter, but he denied in his confession that he killed anyone, although admitting freely that he tried to:

> I drew my pistol and cocked it but somehow it went off prematurely and I shot McMurdy across the thigh, my pistol ball cutting his buckskin pants. McMurdy turned to me and said, 'Brother Lee, keep cool, you are excited. You came near killing me...' Knight then shot a man in the head. Knight also brained a boy that was about fourteen years old...all of the sick and wounded were killed almost instantly. I fully intended to do my part of the killing, but by the time I got over the excitement of the coming so near killing McMurdy, the whole of the killing was done.

All accounts do agree that the killing took but a few minutes. Most of the men of the Fancher party fell at the first volley, the survivors dispatched seconds later. Lee later estimated the total dead at 121, including the three men who had escaped the camp and traveled south toward the Beaver Mountains—they had been found by their campfire and shot—and the three men led by young Aiden.

The Indians stripped the bodies, throwing clothing and dishes from the wagons like children left alone by their parents. The bodies of the Fancher men were searched for valuables, their shoes removed and piled together, and the burial begun. The bodies were dragged together and rude, shallow graves dug for them. Others were rolled into the rifle pits around the Fancher camp and covered with loose dirt.

The young children of the lead wagon were taken to the ranch of church Elder Jacob Hamlin, whose house was closest to the Meadows. Later the children would be distributed among various Mormon familes.

Lee and a few of the other Saints went on later in the day to Hamlin's ranch to eat and spend the night. Lee himself slept soundly on his saddle blanket, using the saddle for a pillow.

The massacre at Mountain Meadows came close to being the only recorded instance of a perfect crime of mass murder. The only witnesses were the perpetrators and they, of course, were not talking. John D. Lee wrote an official report, as Farmer-Agent to the Indians in the southern settlements, placing the entire blame for the incident on the Indians. But that Brigham Young and the Mormon hierarchy knew of the complicity of several Saints in the massacre, there can be little doubt.

By 1859, rumors that white men had taken part in the killing were so rampant that two military parties, one of them from California, the other from Camp Floyd, Utah Territory, and two civilian parties, set out to gather information on the massacre. Their findings pointed toward responsibility for the tragedy at high levels of the church and its membership. Similarly, Justice John M. Cradlebaugh, whose jurisdiction included the southern part of the Territory, also gathered some damaging data, including confessions which named a number of church members present at Mountain Meadows in September 1857. Warrants were issued for the arrest of several of these men but could not be served. The accused had fled and the judge finally had to abandon his efforts.

The massacre eventually became the subject of a variety of doggerel verses and songs, one of which contained these lines:

This life will soon be over and another coming on
And the perpetrators of the deed must suffer for the wrong,
'Tis true they do deny it, and the crime they will disclaim,
To get out of it the best they can, the Indians bear the blame.

By order of old Brigham Young this deed was done, you see,
And the captain of that wicked band was Captain John D. Lee.

But, the Civil War ultimately distracted attention from the massacre—at least for the next decade and a half.

John D. Lee in the late 1860s moved across the southern Utah border into Arizona and established a ferry on the Colorado River, building a small house and clearing a garden. He named the place "Lonely Dell." His complicity in the crime against the Fancher train became dangerously well-known and he had become a serious liability to his church. Thus, in 1870 he received word of his excommunication from the faith he had served with such unwavering zeal for 32 years.

Passage of federal legislation in 1874 outlawed polygamous marriage, ended the theocratic supremacy of the Mormons in Utah and established federal controls over the vast Territory. With these changes came U.S. attorneys granted rights to prosecute, U.S.

marshals to serve and execute writs, and various federal law officers to arrest culprits and bring them to trial.

Lee had traveled from his Lonely Dell to the Utah side of the river to visit his family at Panguitch when, on November 7, 1874, he was taken into custody by William Stokes, a deputy U.S. marshal. The extraordinary fact about Lee's arrest is that he would now stand trial for his role in the Mountain Meadows affair of 1857—and he alone would stand trial.

The case against him opened on July 23, 1875, in Beaver, U.T., but little testimony against Lee had developed—no Mormon, for example, gave evidence against him—and the trial ended in a hung jury, the eight Mormon jurors voting for acquittal, the four Gentiles for conviction. Lee was taken to the Utah State Penitentiary and was released on $15,000 bond on May 11, 1876.

He returned to Panguitch where his wives and sons urged him to flee to Mexico. Lee would have none of it; he had faith that if found guilty, Brigham Young would rescue him—that the church, in other words, would not let him be sacrificed. In this notion, Lee might have remembered the lines from the *Book of Mormon*: "It is better that one should perish than that a whole nation should dwindle in unbelief."

The second trial opened on September 14, 1876, and the intervening year had somehow produced a complete turnabout in the attitude of members of Lee's former church. There were Mormon witnesses arrayed against him who a year before claimed to know nothing. Lee had suddenly and clearly become the Saints' selected scapegoat: it took the all-Mormon jury only an hour, on September 20, to bring in a unanimous guilty verdict. If the first trial had been a farce, the second was a frontier star chamber.

Lee might have escaped the death penalty had he openly confessed and implicated others in the crime of 1857, but he refused, drawing some satisfaction out of writing a memoir of his life and implicating in it Brigham Young and other leading churchmen in various crimes in addition to that at Mountain Meadows. Of himself, Lee wrote: "I have been treacherously betrayed, and sacrificed in the most cowardly manner by those who should have been my friends."

A clemency petition containing the signatures of 514 Utah citizens was presented to Governor G. W. Emery that fall after the verdict, but it had no effect and the execution date was set for March 23, 1877 and the place—perhaps for publicity purposes—

the scene of the horror 20 years before, Mountain Meadows.

Offered his choice of the method of his execution, Lee asked for a firing squad.

It was cool on the morning he would die and Lee, taken under guard with his pine coffin in a wagon to the Meadows, wore a heavy overcoat, muffler and hat. The grassy valley, so lush in 1857, had now given way to a gravelly waste: overgrazing, the floods of 1861 and 1873, and the wagon ruts which helped the erosion, had ruined the once picturesque meadow. The prevailing legend about the ruination was much simpler than this, of course. It said that the blood of the Fancher party had cursed the ground and made it fallow.

Not many paces from the place of execution, nearly 20 years earlier, soldiers had placed a cairn of stones on the Fancher campsite. A cedar cross there bore the words "Vengeance is mine, saith the Lord, I will repay." Brigham Young himself is said to have seen this marker and ordered it removed.

As the five-man firing squad loaded rifles and strode into position, Lee sat calmly on his wooden coffin. He rose and shook hands with all in attendance, removed his hat, coat and muffler and quietly reminded the riflemen to aim at his heart. He permitted a blindfold but asked that his hands remain free. At the signal, the volley rang out and without a sound, Lee fell dead across his coffin.

"Not a particle of mercy have I asked the court, the world, or officials, to spare my life," he had written. "I do not fear death. I shall never go to a worse place than I am now in."

Lee's body was turned over to two of his sons (he claimed 54 children from his total 19 wives) and taken by wagon to Panguitch for burial. For 80 years only a simple stone marked his grave, but on August 11, 1960, his descendants placed a new marker on the plot containing the telling admonition: "Know the Truth and the Truth shall make you free."

A year after this quiet ceremony, Lee was quietly, posthumously, reinstated to membership in the Church of Jesus Christ of Latter-day Saints.

At Mountain Meadows, local residents and the Utah Pioneer Trails and Landmarks Association placed a small monument and plaque near the place where the Fancher train perished. In 1966, the land was purchased by the church and the monument eradicated.

Sources:

No work has been written on the 1857 tragedy at Mountain Meadows that is entirely free of bias and none has enjoyed complete acceptance by historians, although Juanita Brooks' *John Doyle Lee: Zealot-Pioneer-Builder-Scapegoat* (1964), and *The Mountain Meadows Massacre* (1962) are the most often consulted on the episode.

Other sources consulted include:

Josiah F. Gibbs, *The Mountain Meadows Massacre,* 1910. This book was the main source for the chapter on the massacre in Jack London's great synoptic novel, *The Star Rover* (1914).

William Wise, *Massacre at Mountain Meadows,* 1976.

James A. Harden-Hickey

King James I of Trinidad

El Paso, Texas, has known its share of mavericks and miscellaneous square pegs, more than its share.

Some of them were of the whiskey-hoisting, gimlet-eyed, gunslinging variety on both sides of the law, such as Billy the Kid, Wes Hardin, John Selman, Dallas Stoudenmire, Pat Garrett, George Scarborough, Jeff Milton and Bass Outlaw. Others were soldiers of fortune like Tracy Richardson and Sam Dreben. There were revolutionaries like Madero, Villa, Carranza and Orozco, and budding revolutionaries such as John Reed.

Then there were those who used El Paso as a jumping-off place for strange journeys.

Old Ambrose Bierce, for example, passed through the town in 1913 on his way to Mexico where he disappeared forever.

And for Baron James A. Harden-Hickey, King James I of Trinidad, graduate of France's renowned military college, defender of the Catholic faith, Theosophist, novelist, newspaper editor, and expert on suicide, El Paso was a place to write *finis* to a remarkable—more correctly, bizarre—career.

Harden-Hickey, in heart and mind a Second Empire Frenchman and kinsman of Napoleon III, was actually born in San Francisco on December 8, 1854, of one of the city's founding families. His father was an Irishman, a wealthy mine-owner, and his mother French. Harden-Hickey later embroidered his lineage to a fare-thee-well, tracing the Irish side to King Milesius, the French to 16th century nobility, and brazenly included this biographical concoction in a book on French authors he wrote in 1887 which included sketches of De Maupassant, Flaubert and Victor Hugo.

In about 1867, young Harden-Hickey was sent to Paris for his education. His body would journey the world over the next 20 years, his mind would bend—literally—to an incredible array of dreams and schemes, but his spirit would remain to the end of his days in Louis Napoleon's France.

While imbibing the atmosphere of Paris during the last gasps of the Second Empire—the Paris of boulevards and quaint cafes, of Dumas *pere* and *fils*, of Bernhardt and Empress Eugenie—Harden-Hickey left long enough to enter a Jesuit college near

Liege, Belgium, to study law at the University of Leipzig, and, at the age of 19, to enter the celebrated military school of Saint-Cyr, near Versailles, from which he graduated with honors in 1875.

For the next 17 years of his life, until a certain God-forsaken South Atlantic island beckoned and drove him toward a last monomaniacal scheme, Harden-Hickey's days were of infinite variety, troublesome and smooth, creative and destructive, wise and unwise. Mostly they were troublesome, destructive and unwise.

He groped first for a career as artist—sculptor, novelist, painter. He was a failure at all three, although eleven of his novels were published under the name Saint-Patrice in the period 1876-1880, and a young reporter named Richard Harding Davis recalled, many years after Harden-Hickey's death, seeing an exhibit of the strange man's paintings in a New York gallery.

The bulk of the period before his around-the-world voyage, Harden-Hickey spent as a journalist, novelist, duellist, habitue of the Latin Quarter and of the boulevards of Paris. In 1878, as a result of the many pamphlets he wrote in defense of the Catholic Church against attacks by Parisian Republicans, he claimed to have been named a "Baron" of the Catholic Church.

More importantly, he began editing a weekly satirical scandal sheet in Paris called *Le Triboulet*, named for onc of Louis XII's favorite court jesters. It was a fanatically Royalist paper, existing for the sole purpose of promoting the cause of the Count of Chambord, grandson of Charles X of France, to the French throne. In his tenure as editor, according to one source, Harden-Hickey was sued 42 times, fined 300,000 francs, and once was expelled from France for caricaturing high political figures.

The Baron is also said to have issued a standing challenge to his fellow editors in Paris: "Would you prefer to meet me upon the editorial page or in the Bois de Boulogne?" he wrote. Among those who chose the latter alternative were Aurelien Scholle, H. Levenbryon, M. Taine, M. de Lyon, Phillipe Du Bois, and Jean Moreas. It is not known what became of these men, but Harden-Hickey is not known to have been so much as wounded in any of his duels.

In 1878 the Baron married the Countess de Saint-Pery by whom he had two children, a girl and a boy.

In 1887, some time after the death of Chambord, Harden-Hickey divorced himself from the futile Royalist movement and moved to London where, among other things, he met Madame Helena Blavatsky, the jowly high-priestess of Theosophy, threw off his mantle of Catholicism (but retained his honorary title), and adopted Theosophy and Buddhism as his religion.

Sandwiched between these activities, and related to his study of Theosophy, Harden-Hickey, spending freely the inheritance left him by his father, sailed for India to study first-hand the Indian Vedas, Hinduism and Brahminism.

Bound for Cape Horn en route to India, the British merchant vessel *Astoria* was storm-buffeted into seeking refuge behind a small, desolately rocky dot of an island, described by Harden-Hickey as 700 miles off the coast of Brazil, called Trinidad. The island, shown on only the most comprehensive of maps today, is located at coordinates 20° 30′ 32 south latitude, and 29° 50′ west longitude. It is variously listed as Ilha de Trindade, Trinadade, and—in the earliest accounts of voyages in the South Atlantic—as Trinidad o Ascencion.

Little is written in English on the island, but in 1698 one Dr. Halley is said to have visited it and found nothing more remarkable there than land-crabs and sea-turtles. In 1700, Trinidade was settled by a handful of Portuguese from Brazil who left soon afterward and whose stone houses were seen by Harden-Hickey nearly 200 years later. In 1821 a great store of gold and silver plate plundered from Peruvian churches was supposed to have been concealed on the island by pirates.

In 1822 Commodore Owen dropped anchor at the island and found only cormorants, petrels, gannets, and man-of-war birds. And, in 1889, E. F. Knight, a newspaperman who would later represent the *London Morning Post* in the Russo-Japanese War, visited the island to search for the allegedly buried treasure.

The two most noteworthy features of the wart of land called Trinidade are Ponta das Tartarugas—Turtle Point—a jut of land near where the rare visiting vessel dropped anchor, and Pico Trinidade, a peak in the center of the island, 1,952 feet high.

Despite Harden-Hickey's later outrageously contrived description, Trinidad was a depressing no-man's land of rocky ravines, petrified guano deposits, lava flows, low-hanging fogs, and sharp coral ridges.

After exploring the island and before reboarding the *Astoria*, Harden-Hickey planted a makeshift flag and proclaimed Trinidad his own. With barely a backward glance, but with a bizarre scheme

*This is the only known likeness of Harden-Hickey, a sketch from **Real Soldiers of Fortune** by Richard Harding Davis (1906).*

already hatching in his fertile mind, the Baron and the *Astoria* steamed for India.

By 1890, when he returned to France, the Baron had learned Sanscrit, traveled in India, China and Japan, and was ready for a second try at matrimony. The bride, Anna Flagler, was the daughter of an American iron millionaire and Harden-Hickey wasted no time in whittling away at his wife's fortune. He continued his Buddhist studies, finished a book titled *Bible Plagiarisms*, purchased ranch properties in Texas, California and Mexico, and wrote a fantastic tract he called *Euthanasia: the Aesthetics of Suicide*, filled with classical quotations defending suicide and enumerating several methods of accomplishing it.

Harden-Hickey's Trinidad scheme, which became public in November 1893, in a New York newspaper story, was fantastic but no more so, actually, than a dozen other weird episodes in the man's extraordinary career. No one knows how long the scheme germinated. Perhaps it began taking shape the moment he stepped ashore on the desolate island and planted his flag. One is inclined to see the plan forming, detail by detail, as Harden-Hickey explored Trinidad in 1888 as the *Astoria* waited out the storm en route to India.

In a series of public statements, press interviews and stamped, sealed, be-ribboned proclamations, Harden-Hickey not only proclaimed the island as his own (under what he termed "a maxim of international law" which declared that anyone may seize and hold unclaimed waste land), but laid down his plan for promoting, populating and ruling his island principality. From a "chancellery" established in a West 36th Street walk-up flat in New York City, Harden-Hickey (now King James I of Trinidade) said frankly he would rule the island as a military dictatorship, would seek colonists willing to purchase bonds and otherwise invest in the venture, would establish definite social classes of the populace (the aristocracy would pay well for the privilege of being aristocratic), reward efforts in the arts, industry and science, promote such natural resources of the island as its guano, turtles and legendary buried treasure.

Coolie labor would do all the hard work, according to a prospectus the King had printed up, while the aristocracy would "live beautifully." Richard Harding Davis wrote years later that Harden-Hickey not only recruited 400 coolies and fitted out a schooner to take them to the island, but progressed so far as to hire an agent to give tours of the island and to supervise construction of docks and wharves to receive the shiploads of colonists and equipment.

Davis visited the "Chancellerie de la Principaute de Trinidad" which he said was in a "dirty brownstone in a dirty neighborhood just west of Seventh Avenue," and described it in these words: "On its doorstep children of the tenements were playing dolls with clothespins; in the streets a huckster in raucous tones was offering wilted cabbage to women in wrappers leaning from the fire-escapes. The smells and the heat of New York in midsummer rose from the asphalt. It was a far cry to the wind-swept island off the coast of Brazil."

As for Harden-Hickey himself, Davis wrote, "He should have lived in the days of the Three Musketeers. He was absolutely honest, and as absolutely without a sense of humor."

From the "Chancellerie" the Baron showed visitors the official flag of Trinidade—a yellow triangle on red ground—sold his bonds, issued postage-stamps, answered correspondence, promoted his scheme, and watched it all, in all its papier-mache splendor, collapse when, early in 1895, a British warship landed troops on the island for the innocent-seeming purpose of building a wireless cable station there.

To the Baron, the landing was an invasion of his kingdom (and in Brazil it was considered a flagrant provocation, as that country considered the island as its own), but his protests, aside from creating good copy in New York newspapers, was lost in the diplomatic din between Brazil and Britain. The two nations resolved the dispute when the British withdrew its garrison and turned the island over to Brazil, which formally assumed possession.

Harden-Hickey's Trinidad scheme was thus shattered with pathetic suddenness and finality, although the Baron continued to agitate to find a solution that would permit him to establish a monarchy on the island.

Early in 1898, Harden-Hickey traveled to Mexico in an effort to dispose of the ranch property he and his long-suffering wife owned. The idea was, of course, to raise money. Somehow he failed to sell the property.

On the third of February 1898, the Baron returned from Mexico, crossed the Rio Grande at Ciudad Juarez, and entered El Paso. He registered at the Pierson Hotel as "Harden-Hickey, Paris" and for several days wandered about the town, leaving the impression on those he met of a military man, an aristocrat, aloof and elegant, but courteous and of refined manner. He was truly a striking figure in the dusty frontier town: tall, expensively dressed, with a decidedly French manner, military moustache and beard, hair cut in the Napoleonic style—short and coming to a point on the forehead.

At the Pierson, all eyes followed him as he strolled through the lobby and ascended the staircase to his room, Number 35. The Pierson's manager, a Mr. Fisher, and the hotel maids and other employees came to look forward to his courtly, courteous greetings.

It was not surprising then that on February 10, when the distinguished guest failed to appear from his room, suspicion was aroused. At first the room service help rapped on the door and when gaining no response, thought the French visitor merely enjoying a late nap. By noon, however, when Number 35 could not be aroused, someone was appointed by Manager Fisher to peer through the transom into the room.

Harden-Hickey was seen lying motionless on the floor, his eyes wide open. The door was forced, doctors summoned, but the Baron was dead. Following one of the prescriptions in his morbid book on euthanasia, he was a suicide, having apparently taken a heavy overdose of morphine and chloral hydrate.

Among the man's pathetic effects were a note addressed to his wife, a small tin box containing jewelry, medals, the crown he intended wearing as monarch of Trinidade, and a copy of *Euthanasia* which an El Paso newspaper described as "containing a philosophy such as could emanate only from a deceased (sic!) mind."

In addition, there was a letter from one Ralston J. Markowe, lawyer and one-time officer of artillery. The letter showed Harden-Hickey was giving some thought to another scheme as fantastic as any in his life. Markowe outlined a plan by which a group of Hawaiian royalists were intent upon a filibustering expedition to overthrow the Dole government and to restore Queen Liliuokalani to the throne. Harden-Hickey was offered the island of Kauai to rule in return for his services on behalf of the Hawaiian rebels.

The El Paso *Times*, edited by a shrewd newsman named Juan S. Hart, headlined the Baron's suicide as

END OF ALL AMBITION

and ran as the lead sentence these words: "Baron Harden Hickey, the French journalist, duelist, author and ambitious dreamer, is lying dead at the undertaking rooms of Emerson and Berrien." The story ended, "Family troubles and disappointed ambitions were no doubt thorns that goaded Baron Harden Hickey into taking his own life."

The Baron's effects were forwarded to his wife, his remains shipped to San Francisco for burial.

In his book on suicide, he had written: "The wise man lives as long as he ought, not as long as he can," and although he was decidedly not wise, James Aloysius Harden-Hickey, after cutting as weird a swath through life as is imaginable outside books of fiction, apparently decided he had lived about as long as he ought.

Sources:

- Daniel Alden, *Royal Government in Colonial Brazil,* 1968.
- Richard Harding Davis, *Real Soldiers of Fortune*, 1914.
- New York *Tribune*, November 5, 1893.
- El Paso *Times*, February 11, 1898.

William Cowper Brann

The Iconoclast

In his *Desert Island Decameron*, the late H. Allen Smith explained his great admiration for his fellow Illinoisian, William Cowper Brann, the fiery newspaperman of the Gilded Age known by his enemies as the "Apostle of the Devil." Said Smith: "Among the larger pleasures of life, to me at least, is the opportunity of reading vituperative writings. I like the idea of a man getting indignant. . . wiping a bit of the froth from his mouth, then sitting down and shrieking in print. I don't care what he's sore about, and I don't care how far he departs from reason and logic, just so long as his anger is cosmic and his language suited to the voicing of it."

Smith knew his man. Brann was forever sore about something—mostly injustice, the public posturings of the *hoi polloi*, quackery of various kinds, but especially religious and medical; venal and crooked politicians, and ignorance in all its manifold forms. And for a period of about two years, from the pages of his little journal the *Iconoclast*, Brann frothed and shrieked and did it with such sustained brilliance and with such effect that he was shot dead on a Waco, Texas, street by an angered reader.

William Cowper Brann was born in Coles County, Illinois, on January 4, 1855, the son of a Presbyterian minister who admired the melancholy English poet William Cowper. Young Brann's early life was unremarkable except for the variety of jobs he held: bellboy, drummer for a printing firm, painter, printer's devil, fireman on a freight train, and manager of a traveling opera company.

In 1877, in Rochelle, Illinois, Brann married a lovely woman, Carrie Martin. For all their married life, Carrie called her husband by the pet name "Harry."

Brann's newspaper career began in St. Louis in 1883 on the *Globe-Democrat*, a morning Republican paper edited by one Joseph Burbridge McCullagh. This was five years before Joseph Pulitzer bought the *Post-Dispatch* in St. Louis and began retooling American journalism. (Brann would later label this Titan among newspapermen, "Joseph Phewlitzer.")

The *Globe* was the first of a number of newspaper desks for the ambitious, intelligent, temperamental Brann. He moved from St.

Louis to the *Evening Tribune* in Galveston, Texas, and by 1889 was an editorial writer for the *Galveston News.* Still later he moved over to the *Houston Post* and became chief editorial writer there.

The existing evidence seems to indicate that Brann became an itinerant newsman by necessity rather than choice. He was a violently partisan and uninhibited individualist and doubtlessly nearly came to blows with editors of a more traditional nature, and owners fearful of upsetting somebody's applecart.

Brann was almost entirely self-educated and what he knew he got from reading, "the nurse of culture," he said, just as "reflection is the mother of genius."

His vocabulary was an astonishing mixture of Shakespeare, Carlyle, Dante and Tom Paine, with a sprinkling of Swift and Voltaire in his humor and satire. Early in his career, Brann had a reputation as a master wordsmith and few could touch him when it came to knowledge of the language and the sheer stinging force of his use of it.

Brann was never satisfied with newspaper hacking and continually dabbled in "serious" writing, as if seeking a place in a higher pantheon than that available to the journalist. But this was an idle dream. Early in 1889, when he had just passed his 34th birthday, he paid $1.50 to enter three plays in the office of the Librarian of Congress. Of the three—"Retribution," "Cleon," and "That American Woman,"—only the first, a crude melodrama, was ever staged. On June 30, 1893, in the Grand Opera House of San Antonio, "Retribution" was performed. As was customary in honoring a local literary man, the reviews were good, but Brann knew the play was bad.

1890 was a tragic year for Brann and Carrie. Their 13-year-old daughter, Inez, committed suicide on July 25 of the year with an overdose of morphine tablets after a family argument and the awful event gnawed at Brann for the rest of his life. He began seeing himself as an ill-starred, if not tragic, figure.

Soon after Inez's death, Brann launched *The Iconoclast* in Austin, Texas. The idea and the name were pets of his. The journal-newspaper bearing that name (it means, of course, an idol-smasher) would contain irreverent articles and commentary—in brief, it would give Brann a chance to write what he pleased and how he pleased.

As it developed, the *Iconoclast*, even in this early stage, became known (admittedly to a precious few who bought it) for its satire and wit, honed to the razor's edge, slashing to the bone but graceful—even flowery—in its devastating way. Brann's invention in rancor was always staggering. "I long for the power to transform the English tongue into the writhen bolts of Jove," he said of his favorite single target, religious bigots, "and hurl the cowardly and unclean curs to the profoundest depth of hell."

The Austin *Iconoclast* failed, however, before more than a scattered few Jovian bolts, and Brann disposed of his press and few fixtures to a bank teller named William Sidney Porter—later famed as O. Henry.

In 1892, Brann was back on the road. He became editor of the *San Antonio Press* for a short period and in 1894 arrived in Waco where he had been hired as an editorial writer for the *Daily News.*

The town on the Brazos River was called by its civic boosters "The Athens of Texas," and by others "Six-Shooter Depot." Both titles had an element of truth in them. Waco was then the eduational center of the state with Waco Female College, Catholic Academy of the Sacred Heart, Paul Quinn University (for Negroes), and Baylor College, a Baptist school with an enrollment of over 500 students.

Close on the Chisholm Trail, Waco was also a health spa whose artesian wells were advertised widely to cure everything from St. Vitus Dance to locomotor ataxia. The town was also rich in cotton and was the sixth largest city in Texas with a population of 25,000. In 1894, in addition, it shared a distinction with Omaha, Nebraska and El Paso, Texas, of having a sanctioned red-light district. In Waco it was called "the Reservation." There were also many saloons and many churches for the dry and devout.

Brann soon quit the *Daily News* and again launched his *Iconoclast*. The first issue, dated February 1895, was a two-column pamphlet the size of ordinary letter-paper. It sold for 10 cents an issue or $1 a year. The lead editorial in that inaugural issue was deceptively understated: "*The Iconoclast*," Brann wrote, "is simply an independent American journal exercising its Constitutional prerogative to say what seemeth unto it best, without asking any man's permission." He affirmed that he was not "hoping to reform the world" or to "drag the golden age in by the ears, or pull the millenium before it is ripe," only to "recover a few acres of Mother Earth from the domain of Falsehood and Folly."

From the first issue, the *Iconoclast* was a horn of plenty. Its readers were blinded by its brass, deafened by its raucous blast. The subject matter might range from James Whitcomb Riley ("the poetical ass with the three-storey name") to national politics and social mores, from such now obscure issues as the free coinage of silver to bicycling and women's bloomers.

Religion, particularly fundamentalism, was a favorite Brann target. "My bump of reverence is not so large as to wear out the crown of my hat," he wrote, and he began his religious crusade by singling out a malignant organization, long since defunct, called the APA.

The American Protective Association was a violently anti-Catholic assemblage in which traveled renegade defrocked priests and "former nuns" haranguing audiences with sordid tales of popery and designs of world domination by the Catholic Church. Brann immediately renamed them "The Aggregation of Pusillanimous Asses" and "the A. P. Apes," and said, "Of course the APA cannot long survive. It is a Child of Darkness and must perish with the coming of the Dawn. There is no valid reason for its existence, and the law of social, as well as of physical evolution, makes it imperative that the useless and unfit should perish from the earth."

With equal gusto, Brann ambushed renowned preachers. Of DeWitt Talmadge, a widely known syndicated religious writer who appeared in hundreds of newspapers in his day, the Waco editor wrote: "The *Iconoclast* will pay any man $10 who will demonstrate that T. DeWitt Talmadge ever originated an idea, good, bad or indifferent. He is simply a monstrous bag of fetid wind. The man who can find intellectual food in Talmadge's sermons could acquire a case of delirium tremens by drinking the froth out of a pop bottle."

The *Iconoclast's* circulation grew steadily and along with it Brann's reputation. Among the Waco literati, Brann was a delight; among the more strait-laced, Brann was the "Apostle of the Devil." The latter was precisely the kind of repute Brann expected and sought. Today it might be called his "death-wish."

He admitted in print, "I am always getting into trouble. Either my star is evil or my liver is out of its orbit."

Brann was a loner but it is not to be supposed that he was friendless or an outcast. He had charm, social grace and an infectious wit. True, his enemies were growing in number as fast as his list of friends and admirers.

Some examples from Brann's *Iconoclast* columns maintain a

William Cowper Brann at his rolltop desk at the offices of ***The Iconoclast*** *in Waco, Texas, about 1897*

curious similarity to issues dominant in the news even today:

On Jury Trials: "As a rule we get together twelve of the most consummate blockheads in the county—a dime museum of mental freaks—permit them to be further obfuscated by artful counsel, whose business it is to 'make out a case' for or against, as goes the fee, then lock them up until the most obstinate jackass in the corral dominates the herd or compels a compromise. Sometimes there are two or more burros of equal obstinancy. A mis-trial results, and the case goes over to the next term of court. The public loses interest in it—is absorbed in the contemplation of new crimes—and if the culprit is eventually convicted and properly punished the people regard it as a special dispensation of Providence. Punishment, to have a repressive effect, must be not only sure but swift. The law's delay—coupled with its uncertainty—encourages crime."

On National Politics: "We have fallen into the bad habit of making the U.S. Senate an old folks' refuge or asylum for senility, sending to the lower House of Congress pettifogging attorneys who cannot pick up a livelihood by practicing in chicken courts, then accepting for President whatsoever chump is most satisfactory to the plutocrats. It is small wonder that, with such a captain and crew, the ship of state is drifting to the devil. It is small wonder that her precious cargo is appropriated by pirates, that capitol and White House are permeated by Wall Street's subtle perfume."

Other examples of Brann's rollicking, high-handed humor retain their inventive wit despite the transience of their subject matter.

On a rich society matron in New York: "Mrs. Bradley-Martin does not exactly 'look every inch a queen,' her horizontal having developed at the expense of her perpendicular, suggesting the rather robust physique of her father's beer barrels. Still, she is an attractive woman, having the ruddy complexion of an unlicked postage stamp and the go-as-you-please features of a Turkish carpet."

On John Jacob Astor: ". . . the wooden-shod purveyor of green coonskins and odoriferous polecat pelts, Jamaica bug-juice and brummagem jewelry. With a cash capital of one jug of cheap rum and a shirttail full of glass beads, the thrifty Johann Jakob went among the Indians and founded a fortune which enabled him to buy a large slice of Manhattan Island when it was selling at four cents per acre."

On the death of an editor of the *Los Angeles Times:* "I can but wonder what will become of the *Times* editor when the breath leaves his feculent body and death stops the rattling of his abortive brain, for he is unfit for heaven and too foul for hell. He cannot be buried in the earth lest he provoke a pestilence, nor in the sea lest he poison the fish, nor swung in space like Mahomet's coffin lest the circling worlds, in trying to avoid contamination, crash together, wreck the universe, and bring again the noisome reign of Chaos and old Night. The damn rascal seems to be a white elephant of the hands of Deity, and I have some curiosity to know what He will do with it."

Many pages of the *Iconoclast* were simply exercises in calumny. An example of Brann's description of "The Meanest Man" (who was a pastor of a church in Worcester, Mass., and who earned the Apostle's splenetic hatred over a slight hardly worthy of such a fanatical outburst): "Yes, I have found the meanest man in America. His existence confutes the theory of the survival of the fittest and suggests that mankind is merely a malodor. His character casts a shadow on the sun. He has cirrhosis of the soul. His heart is a green worm that feeds on gall. His bowels of compassion are petrified. If his milk of human kindness were churned, the product would be limburger cheese. He has moral strabismus and carries his brains in his belly. His odor of sanctity would give a polecat convulsions. To sit beneath the drippings of his sanctuary were like getting caught in a cataclysm of sheep dip. We have one tree in Texas on which we have hanged 37 better men—and they are all in Hell."

At his best (or worst, depending on where you were standing), Brann, as H. L. Mencken described him, was "a master of invective." He poured it on and heaped it up—sometimes to the point of reverse effect—and made it so readable and vicariously thrilling that the circulation of the *Iconoclast* rose to an incredible 90,000 by 1898.

In the summer of 1895, Brann launched a withering crusade against Baylor College. It marked the beginning of the end for him. The issue ostensibly was the seduction and impending motherhood of a Brazilian student, Antonia Teixiera, age 14.

The case was simply made to order for Brann: The accused father of Antonia's child was the brother-in-law of Baylor's president. However fragile that tie, it was enough for Brann. Antonia, who had been brought to Baylor from Brazil by Baptist missionaries, became, in the pages of the *Iconoclast*, a "Modest little thing," "dove-eyed," "a little wild-flower" who was snatched "from the Papal power, a veritable brand from the burning." Baylor, the accused and his relatives, were malevolent forces in Brann's columns and he admitted he enjoyed exposing such "social ulcers and special sectarian scandals."

Actually Brann had given a far different opinion on the matter of seduction before the Teixiera case arose. He had written: "A woman rightly reared and carefully guarded until she is of marriageable age will never be 'led astray' unless she furnishes the string."

But, of course, Antonia was no woman, only a child.

Brann's attacks on Baylor and what he conceived to be its closet-full of skeletons, continued unrelentingly. He wrote, "Language hath its limits, and even Dante could only liken the horrors of hell to earthly symbols. It were as impossible to describe in print the case of Antonia Teixiera as to etch a discord or paint a stench. Before justice can be done to such a subject, a new language must be invented—a language whose words are coals of juniper-wood, whose sentences are woven with the warp of aspic's fangs and a woof of fire."

In early October 1897, over two years after the Teixiera scandal began, Brann was abducted, trussed up by a gang of toughs who threatened to lynch him, beaten senseless and forced to sign a paper calling himself a liar. A few days later, still recovering from the beating, he was caned and horsewhipped on a Waco street by an irate citizen.

The next month he was back at his roll-top desk, pen in hand, and the lead article in the *Iconoclast* began with spirited humor: "My Baptist brethren desired to send me as a missionary to foreign lands, and their invitation was so urgent, their expressions of regard so fervent, that I am now wearing my head in a sling and trying to write with my left hand." He quickly got down to business and warned: "I'm too slight for a slugger . . . but I can make a shotgun sing 'Come to Christ.' "

Brann's violent encounters with Waco's incensed citizenry troubled Carrie Brann to the point of nervous exhaustion and no doubt gave her husband more than a taste of fear. If fear was present, it was not reflected in the *Iconoclast*, however, and the journal continued as belligerent as ever. At the same time, the temperature of Waco's smouldering townspeople was rising to the boiling point.

Brann reflected on this state of affairs: "People say to me," he wrote, "Brann, your attacks are too harsh. You should use more persuasion and less pizen. Perhaps so; but I have not yet mastered the esoteric of choking a bad dog to death with good butter." And again later he said, "...Never try to move an ox-team with moral suasion, or to drown the cohorts of the devil in the milk of human kindness. It won't work."

The next step in the simmering Brann-versus-Baylor feud was a bloody one. Judge G. B. Gerald, Waco's County Judge and a fire-brand who openly espoused Brann's side of the controversy, published several open letters and handbills in which he viciously attacked—among others—Jim and Bill Harris of the Waco *Times Herald*, staunch defender of the Baylor side of the case. Judge Gerald, on November 19, 1897, fought a three-way duel with the Harris brothers on Waco's busiest street, killing both men and losing an arm himself in the sanguinary gunfight.

By the spring of 1898, the *Iconoclast* proprietor and his wife were preparing for a long-planned vacation, a respite eagerly anticipated by Carrie Brann especially. On April 1, Brann ventured downtown, visited a saloon and walked down a main Waco street with an *Iconoclast* employee. Neither man noticed the furtive figure lunging toward the sidewalk from an office front. The man fired a shot at Brann's back from a distance of barely ten feet. Brann whirled, his own gun, which he habitually carried, in his hand. He methodically fired shot after shot toward the crouching, unknown assailant. Then, his gun emptied, Brann fell to the pavement. The attacker, too, sprawled headlong across the walk. Brann was examined on the street and someone noted that his shoes were filled with blood and a massive wound was blossoming in the middle of his back, "right where the suspenders crossed."

The "Apostle of the Devil" was taken by carriage to his home. His wounds were in the back, foot and groin and at 1:55 a.m., April 2, 1898, he died. In the house he called "the Oaks," its furniture shrouded preparatory to their ill-fated vacation. Brann's long-suffering Carrie and their two children sobbed at his bedside.

The man who killed the *Iconoclast* editor was named Tom Davis and, it was later reported, he had a daughter attending Baylor and had political ambitions. Any combination of these ingredients—and others—could have led to his act, but no one was ever to know for certain. Davis, struck by four of Brann's bullets, died in agony the same day as the shooting.

William Cowper Brann was buried beneath a granite obelisk in

Waco's Oakwood Cemetery. The marker bore a bas-relief likeness of the *Iconoclast* editor, and a stone lamp bearing the word "Truth."

He left something of an epitaph in the pages of his paper when he wrote: "I have striven to break foolish idols and shatter false ideals, to hurl unclean gods from their pedestals in the public pantheon... I do not build the spasmodic sob nor spill the scalding tear because all men are not Sir Galahads in quest of the Holy Grail, and all women angels with two pairs of reversible wings and the aurora borealis for a hatband. I might get lonesome in a world like that."

Sources:

- *Brann the Iconoclast*, a collection of the writings of William Cowper Brann (2 volumes), 1898.
- Charles Carver, *Brann and the Iconoclast,* 1957.
- Roger Conger, ed., *The Best of Brann,* 1967.
- Edward G. Fletcher and Jack L. Hart, *Brann the Playwright,* 1941.
- H. Allen Smith, *The Desert Island Decameron,* 1945.

'Pecos Bill' Shafter

and the War Correspondents

On the morning of June 22, 1898, an American army was preparing to disembark from transport ships lying at anchor off the village of Daiquiri on the southeastern shore of Cuba.

The landing orders by Maj. Gen. William R. Shafter the night before were crystal clear. All persons not immediately on duty with and constituting part of an army unit would remain on board the transports until the landing was accomplished or until notified they could proceed ashore.

Two forces were now in a collision pattern—although as yet the Americans had not met the Spanish foe. On the one hand there was Shafter, in command of 819 officers and 15,000 men, working feverishly on a highly complex and dangerous landing operation in choppy seas toward an unknown terrain and an uncounted enemy. On the other hand there were 89 war correspondents in the expedition, representing America's finest newspapers and magazines, not a few of them 18-karat representatives of that gift of the Golden Age known then as now, as "yellow journalism."

Inevitably, that morning of June 22 there came a confrontation. Shafter was a man with a notoriously short fuse and the person who lit it was none other than Richard Harding Davis, *beau sabreur* among the journalists, dressed in his war correspondent suit: soft felt hat with white puggree, high white collar, blue coat, trousers tucked into tall, spit-polished field boots, binoculars slung rakishly at his side—the Gibson Man, inpeccable and terribly handsome, going to war (and, if William Manchester is correct, going to war wearing silk underwear) for *Scribner's Magazine*. The fates decreed that it would be Dick Davis who would face the 310-pound, gouty and irascible bulk of a man who commanded the army about to land on the Cuban beach.

"General, I see the order for disembarkation directs that none but fighting men may be allowed in the boats of the first landing party," Dapper Dick said, standing before the blue-eyed, shaggy-browed Shafter. "This will keep back reporters."

Shafter allowed that this was true, adding that the sandhills and brush-covered rises behind Daiquiri's beach could be swarming with Spanish snipers and he needed every soldier he could get on shore to hold the position.

The unassailable logic of Shafter's response did not impress Davis who, determined to get ashore with the troops, pointed out to the General that he was no mere reporter but "a descriptive writer." It was at best a weak ploy and Shafter, who would have entertained no change in the landing order short of a direct command from President McKinley, shot back: "I do not give a damn what you are. I'll treat you all alike."

Davis was sorely offended at this rude reply and, it is said, went below deck to sulk in the cabin *Scribner's* had arranged for him. Shafter's assistant adjutant general, E. J. McClernand, who witnessed this incident, later wrote: "So far as I know, Mr. Davis never said a kindly word about General Shafter afterward."

Exactly 25 days after the Daiquiri landing, Shafter had the surrender of Gen. Jose Toral, in command of Spanish forces on the island, and stood in the parade ground of the governor's palace in Santiago de Cuba to see the Stars and Stripes raised to fly over the Cuban capital.

In 25 days, Shafter had moved his army, swollen to 20,000 officers and men, from the Daiquiri beachhead to Siboney, thence toward Santiago by way of the San Juan Hill complex, and finally to the outskirts of the capital itself, the town reverberating under the bombardment of the American Navy off the Santiago Channel.

Along the way, sharp and scary little actions had been fought at Las Guasimas (where Lt. Col. Theodore Roosevelt and the Rough Riders got into trouble—correspondent Stephen Crane flatly called it an "ambush"—with the rearguard of a retiring Spanish force), El Caney, Kettle Hill and San Juan Hill. Shafter, possessing at best imperfect information on enemy defenses and numbers, had landed his troops in open boats on an enemy shore, and in ten days had pushed the Spanish back to their original line of entrenchments, before their own capital city.

In little more than three weeks, the General had compelled the surrender of 11,500 men in Santiago plus another 12,000 Spanish soldiers in outlying positions. Moreover, he had carried out the campaign in Cuba's sickliest season while he himself was prostrate with fever and gout.

Now he stood to watch the flag raised over the enemy capital and, having prohibited the press from the ceremony, had no inkling of what was about to occur.

Several correspondents had defied Shafter's order and were inside the city for the flag-raising. Among them was a pugnacious reporter for the New York *World*, Sylvester Scovel, a man who had been on the island since the early days of its latest rebellion, in 1896, and whose work stands to this day as a puzzling mixture of brilliant reportage and shabby, wholesale fabrication.

Scovel stood, in fact, on the roof of the governor's palace with the American troops awaiting the signal to hoist the flag. Shafter ordered the correspondent down, shouting to Scovel in the familiar thundering oaths that issued from the scarlet-faced General's mouth in times of temper. Reports vary on what took place on the parade ground once Scovel descended, but most agree the *World* writer protested "in a loud voice," this followed by louder imprecations from Shafter. Scovel thereupon threw a wild punch at the General, which apparently, and inexplicably, missed its large target, and was grabbed by Shafter's troopers and hustled off, under arrest, to the nearest Santiago *calabozo*.

(To bring the story full circle, Scovel became *persona non grata* to the army after the incident, and his professional journalistic career was at an end. He maintained, in a letter to President McKinley, that he struck Shafter "in answer to the general's blow," but although many witnessed Scovel's wild punch, no one saw Shafter do anything but bellow. Scovel stayed on in Cuba as a consulting engineer and later as a businessman and died there in 1905.)

Historian Stewart Holbrook, in his book *Lost Men of American History* (1946), summed up the matter of the general's war with journalists simply: "The Yellow Press assassinated Shafter."

From first to last, in the Santiago Campaign of 1898, it amounted to about that. Shafter, with his walrus moustaches, his hair parted down the middle, his short legs and ponderous size, his beet-faced temper and propensity for swearing (". . . under stress, the profanity rolled out of his huge girth like gathering thunder," Holbrook wrote), did not ingratiate him to the press. His attitude toward them, indeed, was that of a shark toward the pilot fish who ride on them and snap up the remnants of their meals: parasites—ignore them.

Shafter hated publicity for himself and "personal glory never entered into his calculations," as Holbrook put it. In his attitude toward self-aggrandizement, Shafter was thrown into contrast with the folk-hero of the campaign, Theodore Roosevelt, colonel of the First U.S. Volunteer Cavalry Regiment (Rough Riders), who was riding on a bee-line from the summit of San Juan Hill to

Gen. William Rufus "Pecos Bill" Shafter

the White House.

Richard Harding Davis, great friend of Roosevelt's, would never, even in the delirium of yellow fever, have written ill of the Colonel or exposed him for the military dilettante, glory-seeker (he campaigned rather too openly for a Medal of Honor, which he neither deserved nor received) and poseur that he was. Roosevelt, on the other hand, had no compunction in saying ill of his commander, being quoted as stating in the pontifical Rooseveltian style, "Not since the campaigns of Crassus against the Parthians has there been so criminally incompetent a general as Shafter."

TR's self-glorification, on the other hand, fooled few besides Davis. In 1899, when Roosevelt published his book *The Rough Riders*, Finley Peter Dunne's irrepressible "Mr. Dooley" said:

> I haven't time f'r to tell ye the wurruk Tiddy did in ar-rmin' an' equippin' himself, how he fed himself, how he steadied himself in battles an' encouraged himself with a few well-chosen worruds whin th' sky was darkest...But if I was him I'd call th' book 'Alone in Cubia.'

In his attitude toward the press, Shafter was hostile, but he was hardly oblivious to the presence of the correspondents. He would have had to be dead not to notice the swarms of newspapermen and self-proclaimed "creative writers" who had gathered in Tampa, Florida, where Shafter massed his army for the invasion of Cuba. Each of these styled himself a military strategist and each, in his dispatches, had already laid out his plan—or that of his editor—of the Santiago Campaign before the transports left the Tampa jetty. Shafter knew who they were and what they were doing, but he had an old-fashioned idea in his head to keep the enemy in the dark as much as possible as to his army's strength and his own plan of battle.

In being a sensible commander who also happened to be a fat general unmesmerized by the glitter of the Richard Harding Davises in his wake, Shafter brought down on his head, among others, the two most influential and irresponsible newspapers of the era, Joseph Pulitzer's New York *World* and William Randolph Hearst's New York *Journal*. Both howled for his removal, charging him with criminal negligence, over-caution, sloth and timidity. These and other papers and periodicals ran cartoons unmercifully caricaturing Shafter's Taft-like bulk and the large carriage he used to move about his lines when incapacitated with gout and fever.

This was not journalism's finest hour, but thus did William Rufus Shafter, born October 16, 1835, as Kalamazoo, Michigan's first native-born white child, languish for a time in the minds of avid newspaper readers. He survived the war by eight years and never spoke of—least of all complained about—the mauling he had endured at the hands of the press. (Indeed, as his correspondence with Secretary of War Russell Alger shows, he went out of his way to see to it that the New York *World* was allowed continued representation in Santiago after Sylvester Scovel had been jailed and expelled.)

Stewart Holbrook considered Shafter one of the "lost men" of American history, and said of the gruff old soldier that he was "quite likely the most cruelly maligned general officer of courage, competence and patriotism in our history."

Shafter, at the outbreak of the Civil War, enlisted in the 7th Michigan Infantry and was mustered into service on August 22, 1861. A year later he was appointed major of the 19th Michigan Infantry, and in June 1863, a promotion to lieutenant-colonel. In April 1864, he received his commission as colonel of the 17th U.S. Regular Infantry and earned his brevet as brigadier general in March 1865. He took part in such battles as Ball's Bluff, Yorktown, West Point, Savage Station, Glendale, Malvern Hill, Fair Oaks (where he was woundcd), and Nashville. In Tennessee, he was taken prisoner and held captive for two months.

After the war, on the recommendation of Gen. George Henry Thomas (the "Rock of Chickamauga"), Shafter was appointed to the 24th Infantry, a noted black regiment, and began a long period of service in isolated frontier posts in the Southwest, including Ft. Davis, Texas, in Apache Indian campaigns. During these years Shafter earned the nickname "Pecos Bill" and compiled an excellent record as a leader of men and a tough fighter, doing so quietly and without fanfare while others—Custer, Terry, Nelson, Miles—were becoming Indian fighting legends.

(Of his 40-year Army career, Shafter looked back on his days in the frontier West with greatest pride. He considered himself a soldier of the West, the Apaches his best foes, and, secretly, he liked the "Pecos Bill" moniker bestowed on him by his admiring troopers.)

On June 12, 1895, Shafter received the most coveted award America gives her fighting men, the Medal of Honor. The Medal was granted, upon the recommendation of Gen. Napoleon J. T.

Dana, for Shafter's valor at Fair Oaks, Virginia, on May 31, 1862. Gen. Dana, at the time in command of the 3rd Brigade, 2nd Division, 2nd Corps, Army of the Potomac, gave this account of Shafter's actions after crossing the Chickahominy:

> (Shafter) left half his command at the crossing and, himself, with the remainder marched towards the field where the fighting was. In the heat of the action which followed, his little command, which was on the left of the brigade, was reduced to about five or six men... During the fighting which followed, Lt. Shafter's horse was killed and himself wounded but he remained on duty in the field until the fighting ceased on the following afternoon, before going to the field hospital.

Significantly, in 1917, when a special Army Board reviewed the Medal lists and examined all 2,625 Army Medals of Honor that had been awarded up to that time, Shafter's Medal for Fair Oaks was *not* one of the 911 Medals the Board decided, having not been "properly awarded," to rescind.

At the time of the declaration of war against Spain, in April 1898, Shafter was in command of an Army department in San Francisco and was summoned to Washington by the War Department to take command of the Santiago expedition.

After the war ended, Shafter returned to San Francisco to resume his old post and in 1901 he retired to make a home with his only child, a daughter, in Bakersfield. He died there on November 12, 1906.

Stewart Holbrook wrote of Shafter as good-humored, even jolly, in private, but gruff and grim to his soldiers and to such civilians as politicians and journalists. "As a commander, he was aggressive enough when he thought he had a superiority of forces or when he figured boldness was tactfully called for," Holbrook wrote, adding: "He considered bloodshed an evil, if a battle could be won without it. He refused to be hurried and as a result saved many hundreds of American lives...(In Cuba) he was often confined to his cot by illness but he nevertheless continued to badger the War Department for better food and equipment for the men."

The novelist Steward Edward White knew Shafter intimately and served as the General's literary executor. White said Shafter was one of the few really noble men he had ever known: "Deeply patriotic in the best sense, thoughtful, generous, and direct in all dealings both private and public."

White added, "Never, although doubtlessly hurt by them, did Shafter mention the name of any reporter or newspaper who had a part in defaming him."

Sources:

• The best source on Shafter's career is to be found in seven rolls of microfilm organized by the Manuscript Division of Stanford University, repository of the Shafter Papers. About 80 percent of this collection consists of correspondence of the period 1862-1904, the remainder includes military papers, orders, reports, rosters, broadsides, maps, cartoons, photos, and miscellaneous printed materials and newspaper clippings, a small portion of which was assembled by Shafter's son-in-law, William H. McKittrick, after the General's death.

• Stewart Holbrook, *Lost Men of American History*, (1946).

In the command tent outside Santiago de Cuba, July 1898, from left, Gen. Joseph "Fightin' Joe" Wheeler, Shafter, Gen. Nelson A. Miles

John Reed

Revolutionary in Mexico

It irked Mabel Dodge to no end that her live-in lover had interests outside the elegant boudoir of her brownstone "salon" at 23 Fifth Avenue, New York City.

She had done everything to keep him happy but John Silas "Jack" Reed, the "Storm Boy" out of Harvard and already a Greenwich Village legend, was forever restless in Mabel's gilded cage, drained by her histrionic quarreling, her fake suicide attempts, her smothering jealousy.

He loved to prowl the mean streets of New York's lower East Side at night—he had a romantic notion about prostitutes, much like Stephen Crane's—and to spend time with cronies at the *Masses* office, where he and Max Eastman ran the magazine and wangled money for radical causes from the guilt-ridden rich.

In her four-volume autobiography, in which she told in rather interminable detail of her four husbands and countless lovers, Mabel Dodge vividly recalled the fall of 1913 when her fling with Jack Reed was about to end. His concentration on the daily newspapers, she said, gave a clear signal he would soon be leaving.

The prospect of revolution intoxicated Reed and the New York papers were filled with stories datelined El Paso and Ciudad Chihuahua, telling of the uprising in Northern Mexico and of its chief mover and shaker, Francisco "Pancho" Villa. The Mexican Revolution had begun at last to capture the attention of the American public—if only because it was now washing up against the U.S. border.

Reed was electrified by it—no matter that it was a revolution not motivated by Marxism, it was a *revolution*—and he got the chance he had been waiting for when Carl Hovey, editor of *Metropolitan Magazine*, then an organ of Socialist reform, called Reed in and asked him to go to Mexico as a correspondent. A few days later, the New York *World* also agreed to print his dispatches.

Thus, armed with press credentials and expense money, Reed kissed Mabel Dodge goodbye and set out for the border.

Mabel, in a delayed reaction, found herself devastated by the separation and took the train to Chicago, intercepted Reed and traveled on with him to El Paso. They took rooms in what she called "a large, ugly hotel"—probably the Paso del Norte—and she quickly became bored with the city while her ebullient lover made preparations to cross the border.

"I looked at the pale blue mountains on the horizon," she wrote in later years," and somehow I couldn't see what I was going to do in El Paso while he was over there, for I saw soon enough I couldn't go with him."

After a few depressing days she returned to New York and their affair ended.

At the time of Reed's arrival in El Paso in December 1913, Victoriano Huerta, the "Bloody Usurper" who had engineered the murder of the spiritual father of the Revolution, Francisco Madero, was running his government from a table littered with cognac bottles at the Cafe Colon in Mexico City. Elsewhere in the country, rebel leaders like Emiliano Zapata in Morelos, Alvaro Obregon in Sonora, and Villa in Chihuahua, doggedly fought against the *Huertista* regime. Meantime, the governor of Coahuila, Venustiano Carranza, had issued a proclamation calling for Huerta's overthrow and announcing himself as "First Chief of the Constitutionalist Army."

But on the border, all eyes were on the "Tiger of the North," Pancho Villa, and his Chihuahuan campaign. In November, Villa had marched his guerilla *soldados* north and had captured Juarez, then marched southward to take Ciudad Chihuahua.

Villa needed to crush the *Huertista* army at Ojinaga, just as he needed to wipe out the federal garrison at Torreon, to come to grips with Huerta's forces. It was these campaigns that drew Jack Reed into the glory and misery of the Mexican Revolution, and to contributing mightily in the making of the Pancho Villa legend.

In El Paso, Reed was put in touch with El Paso *Times* reporter Johnny Roberts, a former Hearst newsman who had reported on Villa when the rebel chief was virtually unknown in the Eastern press. Roberts knew Villa and agreed to help Reed get an interview.

By the first week of December 1913, Reed had made his way to Presidio, the Texas town directly across the Rio Grande from Ojinaga. He was dressed in the best tradition of the Golden Age of the War Correspondent: khakis, flat-brimmed campaign hat, high cavalry boots, a pistol and shell belt buckled around his waist.

Underneath all this gear he was a boyish 27-year-old with an unhandsome but friendly face, a shock of mid-parted brown hair and the gently glowing brown eyes Mabel Dodge so fervently remembered. He was a tireless worker and a frequently brilliant writer.

In Presidio, Reed managed to send a note across the border requesting an interview with Gen. Mercado. The note was intercepted by Gen. Pascual Orozco who replied: "Esteemed and Honored Sir. If you set foot inside Ojinaga, I will stand you sideways against a wall, and with my own hand take great pleasure in shooting furrows in your back."

It was enough to chill the ambitions of almost any correspondent, but Reed, at least according to his own account, waded across the river anyway and, managing to avoid a meeting with Orozco, talked briefly with Mercado—"a fat, pathetic, worried, undecided little man who blubbered and blustered."

For the most part, however, Reed quickly wearied of reporting on the rumors of Villa's army approaching, of the refugees pouring across the Rio Grande, and of watching the gunrunners, agents and munitions salesmen plying their trades amid the turmoil of the border town. He returned to El Paso before Christmas. Villa captured Ojinaga on January 14.

In Juarez, Reed got his first glimpse of Villa's army on the march—2,000 horsemen and 500 infantry maneuvering on the desert. "These were wild men," he wrote, "well fed, clothed, armed and mounted; volunteers instead of conscripts like the Federals. A great bunch, believe me."

And, in Chihuahua City, with Johnny Roberts' help, Reed was permitted an interview with Villa, the first of a score of them he described in a series of seven articles for *Metropolitan*, a series that formed part of his 1914 book, *Insurgent Mexico*.

The interviews form a unique profile of Villa, who warmed up to Reed and gave his life story to the American. Reed, in turn, was totally captivated by the jovial, plain-spoken, lusty, generous "primitive whose motive force was to rescue his people from bondage."

Ever the acutest of reporters, Reed noticed everything: Villa's stiff-legged way of walking, owing to his years on horseback, the grace of his features, the terrible power of expression in his deep brown eyes. Other correspondents, by and large a cynical lot to begin with, could not believe Villa had any other program than one of enriching himself and seizing power, but Reed saw Villa as a fellow idealist, a friend of the poor. Others depicted Villa as a mere Mexican hood; Reed saw in him a Mexican Robin Hood and wrote glowingly of the *jefe's* "simple stroke of the pen" by which he

John Silas Reed

confiscated 17 million acres and innumerable business enterprises of the Terrazas and Creel families.

He told of Villa's "black book" in which were listed the names of oppressors of the poor—Americans, Germans and Englishmen. "Their pages in the black book will be opened when the Constitutionalist government is established in Mexico City," Reed wrote, "and there too, he will settle the account of the Mexican people with the Catholic Church."

Reed reported the revolutionary's views on everything, including some issues in which Villa was clearly ignorant, notably socialism and women's suffrage. (On the latter question, Villa said he was not opposed to it, yet he stated that "women can be crueler and harder than men.") And on his loyalty to Carranza, Villa told Reed flatly, "I am a fighter, not a statesman. I am not educated enough to be president. . . I have told you many times there is no possibility of my becoming president."

But, while on the one hand Reed was extravagant in his praise of Villa, he also knew and reported on the darker side of the "Desert Napoleon." Reed was bothered by the ruthless killing of peon soldiers in Huerta's army and by Villa's attitude that "no peon would volunteer against the cause of liberty unless he were bad," when, in fact, many were conscripts pressed into service and helpless to resist.

Reed was also horrified by the killing of prisoners by Rodolfo Fierro, known as "the Butcher," who, as Reed put it, "killed for the pure joy of it. During the two weeks that I was in Chihuahua, Fierro killed 15 inoffensive citizens in cold blood. But there is a curious relationship between him and Villa. He was Villa's best friend; and Villa loved him like a son and always pardoned him." All this might have been a significant factor to Reed in evaluating Villa's character, but it did not change Reed's overall glowing impression of the man.

During January 1914, when not working, Reed spent his time in the El Cosmopolita bar in Chihuahua City, playing stud poker and drinking Tom and Jerries with Johnny Roberts and the other newspapermen in the city. But, because he was looking for action and good copy, he soon struck south to Jimenez, Magistral and Las Nievas, in northern Durango, to the headquarters of Gen. Tomas Urbina, one of Villa's generals reported to be preparing for a sortie against the *Huertistas* in that vicinity.

At Las Nievas, Reed met Urbina in the general's adobe house, a place swarming with children and animals (the general's baby daughter, Reed noted, was using a rifle cartridge as a teething-ring). Urbina was indeed preparing to march, and Reed obtained permission to join him, riding in the baggage coach with the general's swords, typewriter, uniforms, a 12-gallon demijohn of *sotol* firewater, three boxes of dynamite and a case of grenades.

Reed spent three weeks with Urbina's band, jouncing over hundreds of miles of desert and mountain foothills, sleeping on the ground and dancing and carousing in looted haciendas. It was, he said later, "perhaps the most satisfactory period of my life."

At the outpost of La Cadena, Reed saw his first up-close action with Urbina's small force pitted against a thousand *Huertista* irregulars. The outpost was routed, and Reed joined the panicky flight of Urbina's *soldados*, stripping off his camera, overcoat and any other encumbrances as he sought cover in the desert mesquite bushes.

By the time Reed made his way back to Chihuahua City, Villa was making serious preparations for the advance southeast on Torreon, the town that barred the way to any Constitutionalist offensive against Mexico City. Reed learned that Huerta's commander at Torreon, Gen. Velasco, had fortified the city with a trench network, barbed wire, field gun batteries and machine gun emplacements and had boasted the city was impregnable.

Because there was a lull before this storm, Reed returned to El Paso in February to cover for the *World* the killing of William W. Benton, the hot-tempered Briton who owned ranch and mining properties in Durango. Benton accused *Villistas* of rustling his cattle, and somebody shot Benton. Nobody knew the identity of the murderer, but Rodolfo Fierro's name was commonly mentioned, Reed reported.

After a quick trip over to Nogales on the Arizona border to see Carranza ("You got the impression of a vast, inert body—a statue," Reed wrote in the *World*), he returned to Chihuahua during the first week of March 1914, where correspondents were gathering, along with Villa's *soldados*, their wives, children and camp-followers, for the boxcar descent on Torreon.

On March 16, the troop trains and supply wagons moved out, with Reed and the other newspapermen occupying a boxcar equipped with an icebox, stove and two barrels of beer.

Concentration point for the Torreon attack was at Yermo, 70 miles north of the city where Villa's artillery park had been established. During the probing of the outer defenses of Torreon, Reed reported that Gen. Felipe Angeles, Villa's Chapultepec-trained artillery commander, got the Torreon garrison commander on the telephone. Angeles suggested politely that the city be surrendered. Villa himself called a federal official in Gomez Palacio, on the approaches to Torreon, and told this functionary, "I've covered a lot of territory just to see you fellows."

"Are there many of you up there?" the nervous official asked.

"No, not many," Villa replied. "Just two regiments of artillery and ten thousand *muchachitos* to entertain you."

To Reed, there was something positively eerie about the light-hearted, life-goes-on, attitude of Villa's army at this critical point in the Torreon campaign. "A hundred breakfast fires smoke from the car-tops," Reed wrote, "and the women stood turning their dresses slowly in the sun, chattering and joking. Hundreds of little naked babies danced around, while their mothers lifted up their little clothes to the heat."

On March 23, while Reed was dodging federal shrapnel in the vicinity of Gomez Palacio, *Metropolitan Magazine* ran a large display ad in the New York *Times* heralding him as "America's Kipling" for the work he had already published in the magazine and in the *World.*

Reed witnessed the artillery battle with Velasco's batteries inside Gomez Palacio and followed Villa as he led his regiments in the assault on the town in a surprise night attack. The carnage sickened the correspondent: "Seven windrows of men I counted where seven successive charges failed," he wrote. "The trenches were choked with the bodies of the defenders."

Weak from drinking polluted water, Reed followed Villa's army to Torreon where, for five days, the guerillas drove their assault lines against the defenders of the city. On April 1, fighting block by block, Villa bludgeoned his way to the heart of the city, was pushed back momentarily by a last-gap federal counterattack, but won the battle the next day and wired Carranza that the *federales* were in flight. (Gen. Velasco escaped in a blinding dustorm.)

The battle cost 500 *Villistas* dead, 1,500 wounded.

Reed left the battle zone six days before Torreon fell. He had no stomach for the killing. Bribing a railroad hand for use of a motorized rail car, he made his way to Bermejillo and crossed the border three days before Villa's final assault on the city.

In El Paso, Reed wrote a brilliant account of the battle at Gomez

Palacio and the march on Torreon.

For his three months in Mexico, Reed earned little money but enormous prestige. Walter Lippman (one of Reed's Harvard classmates) said, "The articles he sent back from the Mexican border were as hot as the Mexican desert, and Villa's revolution, till then reported only as a nuisance, began to unfold itself to throngs of moving people in a gorgeous panorama of earth and sky."

Rudyard Kipling was quoted as saying that Reed's "articles in the *Metropolitan* made me see Mexico."

John Dos Passos, in his *U.S.A.*, wrote: "Pancho Villa taught him to write. . . Mexico taught him to write."

And Reed himself, in his autobiographical essay, "Almost Thirty," said: "I made good with these wild fighting men, and with myself. I loved them and I loved the life. I found myself again. I wrote better than I have ever written."

POSTSCRIPT: It was eight months after his return from Mexico that Jack Reed met Louise Bryant Trullinger in Portland, his hometown, and began not only his greatest love affair but the last, frenetic phase of his turbulent life. This phase resulted in the classic eyewitness account of the Russian Revolution, ***Ten Days That Shook the World***, and ended with his death on October 17, 1920, three days before his 33rd birthday. He was buried at the foot of the Kremlin Wall in Moscow's Red Square.

Sources:

- Granville Hicks, *John Reed: The Making of a Revolutionary*, 1936.
- Mabel Dodge Luhan, *Movers and Shakers*, 1936.
- Richard O'Connor and Dale L. Walker, *The Lost Revolutionary: A Biography of John Reed*, 1967.
- John Reed, *Insurgent Mexico*, 1914.

Ambrose Bierce

The Devil's Lexicographer

November, said Ambrose Bierce in *The Devil's Dictionary*, is "the eleventh twelfth of a weariness." And, eleven-twelfths weary, Bierce crossed the U.S.-Mexico border in November 1913, never to be seen again.

Probably no similar mystery in American history is so intriguing as the "[1914?]" that follows reference book entries on Bierce. Neither the disappearance of Charley Ross (1874) nor that of Judge Crater (1930) can match the now unfathomable circumstances of Bierce's seemingly well-planned decision to vanish inside revolution-torn Mexico—an ending which, he said, "beats old age or falling down the cellar stairs."

Some writers, including biographer Richard O'Connor, maintain that Bierce's chief claim to fame today is the bracketed question mark after the supposed year of his death. Others balance this by insisting that at least two of Bierce's books deserve lasting fame: *Tales of Soldiers and Civilians* (1891) and *The Devil's Dictionary* (1911). H. L. Mencken, who knew Bierce briefly, eulogized the old newspaperman as the first writer to depict war realistically, in all its horror, waste and uselessness. Mencken, a natural disciple, also called Bierce's epigrams "some of the most gorgeous witticisms in the English language."

Still others, more sensation-minded, say, with more than a little latitude, that Ambrose Bierce was the only journalist ever to be accused of contributing to the assassination of a president of the United States.

The testimony about Bierce is varied—from orotund and effusive (such as that of his publisher and biographer Walter Neale, and Bierce's sometime friend, also a biographer, Adolphe Danziger de Castro), to fair if slightly deprecatory, and full-circle to the view that he is "unimportant," at best a mordant footnote to American literature.

But to those who faintly recognize his name and wonder about that "[1914?]" following his brief biographical entry in reference works, it is natural to ask not only "What happened to him?" but "Who was he?"

Ambrose Gwinett Bierce was born at a place called Horse Cave

Creek in Meigs County, Ohio, on June 24, 1842. He had eleven brothers and sisters, all of them with names beginning with the letter "A"—Abigail, Addison, Aurelius, Amelia, Ann, Augustus, Andrew, Almeda, Albert, Arthur and Aurelia. Ambrose, therefore, began life by hating his name (his middle one as well), and when he later began his rise to fame as "The Wickedest Man in San Francisco," he wrote under the name of A. G. Bierce and showed no dismay when someone translated this to mean "Almighty God Bierce."

Judging from his frequent writings about parenticide, Ambrose also disliked his mother and father, although the father, Marcus Aurelius Bierce, was a bookish man who apparently provided his children an opportunity to know something about literature and culture, both normally far removed from the hard-scrabbled life on an Ohio dirt farm.

At the age of 18, Ambrose joined the Ninth Indiana Infantry, first as a drummer-boy, and fought through some of the bloodiest engagements of the Civil War: Shiloh, Chickamauga, Murfreesboro, Franklin and Nashville. At Kenesaw Mountain in Georgia, on June 23, 1864, he suffered a severe wound—a ball struck him in the head and became embedded among fragments of cranial bone. He recovered, but his brother Albert would later say, "He was never the same after that wound in the head. Some of the iron of the shell seemed to stick in his brain and he became bitter and suspicious."

A year later, Ambrose received his discharge as a first lieutenant, and after a brief time as custodian of captured and abandoned property in Selma, Alabama, he traveled west to San Francisco and took a menial job there as janitor and night watchman at the U.S. Mint. He also began to write.

San Francisco in the late '60s and early '70s, when Bierce began making his career there, had a reputation as a literary, literate city. Bret Harte, Mark Twain, Charles Warren Stoddard, Ina Coolbrith, Prentice Mulford, and lesser lights such as the swashbuckling poet Joaquin Miller, were all considered San Franciscans. The town read its newspapers and magazines and knew its writers.

Bierce's rise, in San Francisco literary circles, to the title his protege George Sterling gave him—"Rhadamanthus of Letters" (Rhadamanthus being the Greek judge of the underworld)—began innocently enough with contributions of scraps of verse and cartoons to such journals as the *Californian*, the *News-Letter*, the

Golden Era, the *Alta California*, and *The Overland Monthly*.

The new contributor had a knack for polished prose and stinging little quatrains, and he had an absolute genius for iconoclastic humor—sometimes in the manner of barbed observations on news and foibles of the day, sometimes deceptively cloaked character assassination, sometimes velvet-covered sledgehammer critiques of nearly anyone's literary efforts. His enemies (whose legions grew in direct ratio to his own notoriety) accused him of being incapable of writing poetry or novels himself while devoting a career to mercilessly attacking such works by others.

Bierce was an exceptionally handsome man: six feet tall, militarily erect, with reddish-blond brows, flowing blond hair and moustaches, and penetrating blue eyes. He was almost inordinately well-groomed and clean. "Ambrose looks as if he shaved all over every day," a wag said of him.

On Christmas Day 1871, Bierce married Ellen "Mollie" Day, the daughter of a mining engineer. Marriage, he would later declare, "is the state or condition of a community consisting of a master, a mistress, and two slaves, making in all, two." And a bride, he wrote, is "a woman with a fine prospect of happiness behind her." While both epigrams were post-mortems to his own marriage, there is little reason to suppose Bierce thought differently at the time he yielded to the temptations of matrimony. The marriage was destined, for master, mistress, both slaves and their progeny, to yield little but unhappiness.

"Here's to woman!" he said in one of the most memorable toasts ever offered. "Would that we could fall into her arms without falling into her hands!"

Bierce sojourned in London between 1872 and 1875, and there he sold his initial literary efforts to the magazine *Fun*, edited by Tom Hood, son of the celebrated "Song of the Shirt" poet. And, using the gloomy pseudonym "Dod Grile," he published three books in England: *The Fiend's Delight* (1872), *Nuggets and Dust* (1872), and another with the ingenious title *Cobwebs From an Empty Skull* (1874).

On the basis of his growing reputation as a satirist, he was also asked to edit a magazine called *The Lantern*, subsidized by the exiled Empress Eugenie of France and intended as an opponent journal of *La Lanterne*, edited by Victor Henri Rochefort, Marquis de Rochefort-Lucay, a violent nationalist and opponent of Napoleon III and the Second Empire. After editing two issues of

The Lantern, Bierce was fired, legend has it, for refusing Eugenie's royal command that he come for an audience with her.

In 1875 he returned to San Francisco a few months behind Day and Leigh, his two children born in England, and Mollie, who was pregnant with a third child. Daughter Helen was born in October of that year, shortly after the Bierces resumed their residency on the Bay.

Bierce was now treated as something of a celebrity—a book writer—and began contributing to the San Francisco *Call,* the *Wasp,* and the *Argonaut.* Aside from a brief time he spent chasing the gold scent in the Black Hills, he devoted his time to freelancing, writing a newspaper column called "Prattle," and developing his craft and reputation as political, social and literary arbiter of the city.

In 1887, Bierce was sought out by the son of one of the city's richest Comstock Lode miners, a horse-faced youngster recently booted out of Harvard, William Randolph Hearst. Young Hearst, upon returning home from the halls of ivy, had been asked what he wanted to do and (heady with inspiration from his brief stint as reporter on the great Joseph Pulitzer's New York *World*) had told his father he wanted a newspaper. George Hearst gave him one—the San Francisco *Examiner*, which the elder Hearst had purchased in 1880 to help further his political ambitions.

The reedy-voiced Hearst had a remarkable talent for organization, and in revamping the *Examiner* to suit his own ideas of journalism (thereby revamping the entire direction of American journalism), he hired the best writers he could find and, in some special cases, went so far as to personally seek out those whom he respected most. Bierce was one of these, and in March 1887, Hearst found Bierce in the latter's Oakland apartment, made an offer that Ambrose could not turn down, and hired the increasingly misanthropic writer on the spot.

Bierce was to become a festering thorn in the side of the ambitious young newspaperman, quitting Hearst's employ uncountable times—always to be wooed back. Bierce, who spoke of Hearst's "fragrance of violets voice," detested and distrusted his employer throughout their long association, but even though the younger Hearst's political aspirations were later shattered with Bierce's aid, there is no record of any enmity on anybody's part except Ambrose's.

On February 4, 1900, a verse that could claim at least some

responsibility for Hearst's political demise appeared in the pages of the owner's New York *Journal.* The occasion was the murder of William Goebel, governor-elect of Kentucky, who had been killed in a political quarrel. Bierce, following his boss's footsteps in attacking the incumbent president, William McKinley, offered this malicious quatrain to the *Journal* readers:

The bullet that pierced Goebel's breast
Cannot be found in all the West;
Good reason: it is speeding here
To stretch McKinley on his bier.

After McKinley's assassination 20 months later, Hearst (and to a lesser degree, Bierce) was accused of helping plant the seed of murder in the mind of McKinley's killer, Leon Czolgosz. Czolgosz, it was said, carried a copy of the *Journal* with him when he left for Buffalo and his fatal rendezvous with the president. It mattered little to Hearst's enemies that Czolgosz had done no such thing and admitted that his twisted inspiration came directly from the preachings of anarchist Emma Goldman.

In Hearst's *Examiner*, though, Bierce's "Prattle" column won instant popularity. Therein Bierce found elbow room for his flail and punished institution and individual without mercy—most often in hilarious fashion, occasionally so venomously it became obvious to many that the scathing, libelous attacks bordered on the pathological. In "Prattle," too, Bierce gave birth to the epigrams that would form *The Cynic's Word-Book*, later expanded into *The Devil's Dictionary.*

In 1896, Hearst called Bierce to Washington, D.C., to cover the story of the Southern Pacific Funding Bill, proposed by magnate Collis P. Huntington to delay the payment of his railroad's $60-$75 million debt to the government. Though one would imagine the capital's climate to have been deleterious to his asthma problem, Bierce liked the city (probably because of its proximity to the Civil War battlefields he had grown to revere) and decided to stay, at the age of 55, to write for Hearst.

If Bierce ever admitted to any happiness before the beginning of the new century, in all probability it was in reflecting on his Civil War days. Despite the horror he described so eloquently in his stories of the war ("An Occurrence at Owl Creek Bridge," "A Horseman in the Sky," "Chickamauga," and others), there is little doubt that, like many an old warrior, he longed for the excitement and turmoil of battle, of the hard camp life, of tests of courage and the chance to demonstrate valor (which he defined as "a soldier's compound of vanity, duty and the gambler's hope.")

But whatever happiness he had in recalling his soldier's life of 35 years past, the new century opened for him with tragedy and disillusionment.

Bierce's marriage to Mollie Day had been a failure from start, and his two sons—Day and Leigh—seemed destined to follow a dismal path. Day broke away from the fold early, in 1889 at the age of 16, to try his hand at reporting on a small newspaper in Red Bluff, California. That same year he became involved in an adolescent love-triangle that resulted in Day's killing the husband of the girl he loved, and then himself. The tragedy effected no reconciliation between Bierce and Mollie.

Leigh Bierce followed his father east and went to work on the New York *Morning Telegraph* (its sports section edited by William Barclay "Bat" Masterson). Leigh, like his father, developed into an "eminent tankardman"; but, whereas his father was never known to be drunk, Leigh's uproarious binges became legend, even on booze-soaked Park Row. After one such bout with the bottle, Leigh contracted pneumonia and, on March 31, 1901, at the age of 27, he died.

Walter Neale, a close friend of Bierce's and his publisher, said the writer's hair turned white a few weeks after Leigh's death.

In April 1905, just before their divorce decree could be granted, Mollie Day Bierce also died—of heart failure.

Bierce carried on his work for Hearst, despite his frequently stated disgust for his employer's favorite journalistic hue—bright yellow. Then, in 1909, Bierce retired to edit his *Collected Works*, a 12-volume publishing venture that was to prove a paste-pot-and-scissors failure, despite the occasional glimmer of literary gold that could be found among the dross. "Fardels of heartache, burdens of old sins, luggage sent down from dim ancestral inns," Bierce had written in an earlier book, "and bales of fantasy from No-Man's Land."

In 1912, the *Collected Works* completed, Bierce began to plan an appropriate final chapter to another work—his own life story.

He planned, to begin with, to visit the battlefields of his youth. He spoke, too, of wanting to make a trip, on foot and burro, across

This 1904 pencil sketch of Ambrose Bierce by Soule Campbell is considered an excellent likeness; Bierce himself must have approved of it for he signed it.

the Cordilleras of the southern Andes, starting out from Santiago de Chile, entering western Argentina, and ending up in Buenos Aires. It was a fantastic notion for a man of 70, but as late as September 1913, he wrote about the South American trek, to be made via Mexico, "...if I can get through without being stood up against a wall and shot as a gringo. But this is better than dying in bed, is it not?"

To his publisher Walter Neale, Bierce spoke almost longingly of finding death in some remote place—the vastness of Grand Canyon or the Yosemite Valley. But the word *Mexico* recurred in his final correspondence and conversation more than the name of any other place.

He left Washington in June 1913, and returned to California where he spent the summer. In September he returned east, stopping off in Bloomington, Illinois, to visit his daughter Helen and to leave some papers for safekeeping. On September 13 he wrote his niece Lora, "Yes, I shall go into Mexico with a pretty definite purpose, not at present disclosable... You must forgive me my obstinacy in not perishing where I am."

Then he moved on to Washington and from there southward, visiting the Civil War battlefields he had known nearly a half-century earlier. On October 24 he stopped in New Orleans where an enterprising reporter interviewed him and quoted him as saying, "I'm on my way to Mexico because I like the game...there are many things that might happen between now and when I come back. My trip might take several years, and I'm an old man now."

To his daughter he wrote, "Why should I remain in a country that is on the eve of prohibition and women's suffrage? In America you can't go east or west anymore, or north; the only escape is south...I'll take some letters of introduction with me and strike the border near El Paso. It will be easy enough to get along. I'm going to buy a donkey and hire a peon. I can see what's doing; perhaps write a few articles about the situation; and then pass to the West Coast of Mexico. From there I can go to South America; cross the Andes and ship to England. This fighting in Mexico interests me. I want to go down and see if these Mexicans can shoot straight."

By late October, Bierce had pushed onto San Antonio where he was feted at Fort Sam Houston by an old army friend. By November 6 he had arrived in Laredo, jumping-off place for the revolution, and from there he wrote to his niece: "There is a good deal of fighting going on over the Mexican side of the Rio Grande; but I hold to my intention to go into Mexico, if I can. In the character of an innocent bystander, I ought to be fairly safe, if I don't have too much money on me, don't you think? My eventual destination is South America; but probably I shall not get there this year."

In another letter that day, Bierce wrote, "...Nuevo Laredo opposite (on the Mexican side), is being held by Huertistas, and Americans don't go over there. In fact, a guard on the bridge will not let them. So those that sneak across have to wade (it can be done almost anywhere), and go at night...I don't know where I shall go next. Guess it doesn't matter much. Adios, Ambrose."

Perhaps a month later, Bierce crossed the border at El Paso into Juarez and journeyed by rail to Chihuahua City, arriving there on December 16, just a few days after the town had been occupied by the soldiers of Francisco "Pancho" Villa. On Christmas Eve, Bierce wrote to a friend, J. H. Dunnigan, "Pray for me—real loud."

The last word anyone heard from Bierce was a letter, dated December 26, that he sent to his former secretary, Carrie Christiansen in Washington. On orders from Bierce, she destroyed the letter—along with most of his other correspondence—but she remembered its contents: "Trainloads of troops leaving Chihuahua every day. Expect next day to go to Ojinaga, partly by rail."

Only silence followed.

Many years after Bierce's disappearance, H. L. Mencken wrote: "When grown old and weary, he departed for Mexico, and there—if legend is to be believed—marched into the revolution then going on, and had himself shot, there was certainly nothing in the transaction to surprise his acquaintances. The whole thing was typically Biercean. He died happy, one may be sure, if his executioners made a botch of dispatching him—if there was a flash of the grotesque at the end." Death, Mencken said, was to Bierce "not something repulsive, but a sort of low comedy—the last act of a squalid and rib-rocking buffoonery."

Bierce did indeed often speak of his belief that a person sometimes reaches the point when he should not wait for death to seek him out. In an essay in *The Shadow on the Dial* (1909), for instance, he argued, "The time to quit is when you have lost a big stake, your fool hope of eventual success, your fortitude and your love of the game."

After the letter Carrie Christiansen is supposed to have received from Chihuahua City on December 26, there is no *real* trail to follow. The battle for Ojinaga (across the U.S. border from Presidio, Texas, 125 miles northeast of Chihuahua) started on January 1, 1915, with Villa's forces, commanded by Gen. Ortega, taking severe losses for the first six days. On January 7, Villa himself arrived on the scene, and by the 10th the federal garrison at Ojinaga, about 4,000 men, had slipped across the Rio Grande for internment in the U.S. As the late Tom Mahoney believed (and stated in his article on Bierce in the February 1936, issue of *Esquire*), Bierce may have joined the Villistas in the Ojinaga battle as an observer and may have been killed there. Mahoney believed Bierce's body, along with those of many soldiers who fell, was burned in open cremation.

The late Prof. Haldeen Braddy of the University of Texas at El Paso, a long-time student of Bierce and his disappearance, wrote that Mahoney's version of the story is "by all odds the most exciting," but added, "The great advantage of this report over all others is that it successfully removes any possibility of a *corpus delicti.*"

Many months after Bierce's last message, his daughter Helen appealed to the U.S. State Department for help in locating her father. Gen. Frederick Funston, in charge of army troops in Texas, was instructed to conduct an investigation into the matter, but this effort turned up nothing of value.

After Venustiano Carranza succeeded the deposed Victoriano Huerta in the Mexico City government, Carranza's investigator, a Maj. Gaston de Pridu, showed Bierce's photograph to many officers in Gen. Ortega's Ojinaga detachment of Villa's army. One man, Capt. Salvador Ibarra, identified it and said Bierce had accompanied the Ortega forces to Ojinaga but that he did not know what happened to the American after that.

Of all the strange and tortuous "leads" that cropped up after Bierce vanished, none is stranger than the story that appeared in the New York *Sun* in the spring of 1915. The *Sun* reported that Helen Bierce, in Bloomington, Illinois, had received a letter from her father which said he was a member of the staff of Lord H. H. Kitchener, then England's war minister, and that he had seen front-line duty in France.

The only particle of evidence connecting Bierce and the great British field marshal, biographer Richard O'Connor claims, is that Bierce began a correspondence with Kitchener in 1899 when the Boer War broke out in South Africa.

The Washington *Post*, on April 4, 1915, asked Helen Bierce to let them publish a facsimile of the "letter" and she allegedly refused. On December 1, 1916, Helen Bierce wrote to Walter Neale stating, "How my father would have enjoyed this European War!" It is scarcely a statement that Helen Bierce would have made had she believed—or, in fact, received—the astonishing revelation about her father. Neale himself said he was never able to confirm the existence of the fabulous letter.

Still another far-fetched rumor, published in *The Bookman* in August 1925, placed Bierce in Lincolnshire, England, in the beginning months of the war in Europe, and said he was training with British soldiers at that time and that he died later in battle on the French front.

It is difficult, of course, to visualize the 72-year-old Bierce training with soldiers in Lincolnshire and being thrown into battle anywhere, as it is to see him on Kitchener's staff—or in Pancho Villa's army.

The Kitchener-Lincolnshire hoax is on a par with the rumors that Bierce spent the last years of his life in a lunatic asylum in Napa, California, attended by his "faithful secretary," George Sterling, and perhaps only a step above the story that circulated in April 1932 in Buenos Aires. This one quoted an explorer named Johnson as alleging to have met "in the unexplored jungles of the Matto Grosso of western Brazil, with a strange man who has long-flowing hair, and who is clad in jaguar skins." The Buenos Aires report continued, "He is being held as a prisoner by a tribe of Indians who look upon him as a god, and have mounted a guard to see that he does not escape. This strange man gave me letters which we lost in our wanderings in the forests. I think he is the lost American writer, Ambrose Bierce."

He may have been, but Bierce, an asthmatic, would have been exceedingly lucky to survive the heat and disease of the Matto Grosso up to the age of 90. Still, the image of him being worshipped as a god is something one hates to relinquish.

Certainly the most intriguing theory on Bierce's fate is that of the San Francisco writer-publisher Sibley S. Morrill. Morrill, in his 1972 book, *Ambrose Bierce, F. A. Mitchell-Hedges and the Crystal*

Skull, places Bierce and the British adventurer Mitchell-Hedges as intelligence agents in Mexico during the Revolution and couples them with the fabled crystal skull of the Maya.

Of all the stories, the most credible place Bierce in Mexico at the time of his death. These versions vary only in *how* he is supposed to have died.

In one account, correspondent George F. Weeks interviewed one Dr. Edmundo Malero of Mexico City, who claimed he knew Bierce well. Malero stated that Bierce originally had joined the Villistas in Chihuahua but deserted to the Carranza camp and had later been captured by Villista Gen. Urbina near the town of Icamole, about 110 miles east of Torreon. Bierce, said Malero, was executed and buried in a shallow grave. Malero, according to Weeks, is said to have later brought one of Urbina's lieutenants to Weeks to confirm the story. The lieutenant is supposed to have identified a photograph of Bierce and confirmed Malero's account.

It is valuable to note that correspondent John Reed, in Mexico in 1913-14 reporting for *Metropolitan Magazine*, knew Villa well and spent considerable time interviewing the rebel general, knew Villa's murderous henchman Rodolfo Fierro, had been present at the battle of Ojinaga, and later interviewed Gen. Urbina. Reed makes no mention of Ambrose Bierce anywhere in his writings. This daring, shrewd and gifted reporter and writer surely knew of Bierce and would have heard, probably in Villa's Chihuahua City encampments, if any American, particularly an American as well-known as Bierce, had died in the Ojinaga battle or been executed by one of Villa's generals.

Another version of Bierce's demise was proposed by Dr. Adolphe Danziger de Castro, with whom Bierce collaborated on the book *The Monk and the Hangman's Daughter* (1893). De Castro was in Mexico in 1922 and said he talked with Villa at the general's great Canutillo ranch near Chihuahua. Villa reportedly became greatly annoyed when Bierce's name was mentioned but proceeded to tell De Castro the story: Bierce was in Chihuahua when the town was captured and the *viejo Americano* got drunk and criticized Villa and his men. Pancho thereupon ordered Bierce expelled from the state and later arranged to have Bierce ambushed, killed and left to the vultures.

Prof. Haldeen Braddy interviewed De Castro in 1929 and wrote, "He was not at all certain that Bierce had actually been murdered at Villa's command." De Castro, in his *Portrait of Ambrose Bierce*

(1929), implies that the old man's death was probably hastened by excessive drinking.

Of all the various accounts placing Bierce with Villa, the most detailed is that of Elias L. Torres, a Mexican mining engineer, writer, and brother of a governor of one of the Mexican states. Torres wrote of Bierce in his book *20 Vibrantes Episodios de la Vida de Villa* ("Twenty Exciting Episodes in the Life of Villa"), published in Mexico City in 1934. The author, in the chapter titled "El Chiste de la Muerte" ("The Joke of Death"), says he (Torres) interviewed Villa at the general's Canutillo ranch and that Villa admitted knowing Bierce well, saying the old man was a frequent visitor to the Villista camp and at Pancho's dinner table. More importantly, Villa told Torres the circumstances of Bierce's death.

According to Torres, Villa claimed that Bierce, during a meal with Villa and his staff officers, denounced the rebel army as a band of thieves and assassins and announced he was abandoning Villa to join Carranza. Villa said he made a sign to one of his officers, Borunda, who quietly left the room. Meantime, Villa told Bierce he was sorry for the decision he had made, gave the old man an *abrazo* (hug), and Bierce left. A few minutes later Bierce and his *mozo* (servant) were heard riding off in the direction of the mountains. Suddenly shots rang out. Villa smiled and addressed himself to his bodyguard, "Butcher" Fierro: "Let's see if that damned *gringo* tells his last joke to the buzzards on the mountain."

Biographer and historian Edward Larocque Tinker, who knew Villa during the Revolution and who lived in Villa's military train, completely subscribed to Torres's story: "That this account is true," Tinker wrote, "I have no doubt. As I have said, it comes to us from a trustworthy source, and every detail is in complete accord with the characters of both Villa and Bierce. . . What I saw and heard persuaded me that he (Villa) would think no more of killing a man than a housewife would of stepping on a cockroach."

Prof. Braddy, who spent years tracing Bierce's final footsteps, said he never uncovered the slightest real evidence of Bierce's fate. Braddy's travels into Mexico, interviews with former Villistas, with Villa's widow, with various soldiers-of-fortune who fought with Villa, yielded nothing of substance. The Texas professor, the most honest and pragmatic of all the Bierce researchers, said, "It is my conclusion that the spreading belief that Bierce died in Mexico rests on no substantial proof whatsoever and should thus be strongly opposed."

Prof. Braddy admitted only this: "In the Revolution of that day, disappearances occurred often and usually without notice. Moreover, Bierce seemed bent on self-destruction and openly said so. My present thought is that Villa did not murder this *Americano*, whose disappearance must rank among the greatest of mysteries. I rather think that age and alcohol together with likely privation and possible exposure to the elements account for his end."

Edward H. Smith, in the book *Mysteries of the Missing* (1927), says, "My own guess is that he started out to fight battles and shoulder hardships as he had done as a boy, somehow believing that a tough spirit would carry him through. Wounded or stricken with disease, he probably lay down in some pesthouse of a hospital, some troop train filled with other stricken men. Or he may have crawled off to some waterhole and died, with nothing more articulate than the winds and the stars for witness."

In his *The Mauve Decade* (1926), Thomas Beer wrote, "If it is true that they shot him against a wall in Mexico, some literate member of the firing-party heard a last pungency and the old man buttoned his coat and faced the rifles, smiling."

And the late Richard O'Connor, a significant Bierce biographer, supported the idea of the old man having the last laugh. In a letter to this writer, O'Connor observed, "I like to think that Bierce ended up in some Andean village, laughing his head off at having completed his most successful hoax."

Sources:

In addition to those sources named in this story and in addition to Bierce's own works, the following books were consulted:

- Allen Churchill, *They Never Came Back* (1960).
- Paul Fatout, *The Devil's Lexicographer* (1951).
- C. Hartley Grattan, *Bitter Bierce* (1929).
- H. L. Mencken, *A Mencken Chrestomathy* (1956).
- Edward H. Smith, *Mysteries of the Missing* (1927).
- Vincent Starrett, *Buried Caesars* (1923).
- W. A. Swanberg, *Citizen Hearst* (1961).
- Robert A. Wiggin, *Ambrose Bierce* (1964).

Tracy Richardson

Machine-gun for Hire

Late in his life, the great American soldier of fortune Tracy Richardson compiled a "personal history." The document consisted of two closely-typed pages with a rubber-stamped "Tracy Richardson, Lt. Col., Air Corps, Commanding," at the end.

It is a strangely laconic paper from a man who fought under the flags of at least seven nations and who carried 16 wound scars on his body—each with its harrowing tale of bullet, shell, bayonet and machete attack. Richardson's two-page life summary contrasts sharply, too, with the way the normally-staid New York *Times* had waxed so eloquently about him; for example, this in 1915:

> Wherever the cannon booms and the rifles bark, this American boy, who embodies in real life the type of moving picture hero one reads about but never sees, is pretty sure to turn up sooner or later—and it is generally sooner. Along the Rio Grande he is known by thousands of the adventurous souls who populate that picturesque and very troublesome stretch of territory. From Brownsville to Nogales there is not a dugout or an adobe but that does not know him.

In contrast, Tracy's own little autobiography trails off thusly:

"I have never used an assumed name.

"I have never been a gambler-professional.

"I have never been expelled from any country.

"I have never been convicted of a crime."

And even aside from its undue brevity, Tracy Richardson's lackluster compilation of data on his fabulous career contains at least one oversight. When he wrote "I have never been a gambler-professional," he was obviously thinking in terms of dice, cards, roulette and such, for he *was* indeed a "gambler-professional"—gambling in banana republics in Central and South America, in Mexico, and in France, that a man with an expert hand on a machine-gun can *survive.*

That Tracy did survive is incredible on the face of it. He survived wars on small and grand scales; lived through rebellion, revolution, and obscure but bloody battle without number; he ran headlong into trouble even when he did not seek it out—such as the occasion when he single-handedly captured the city of Managua, Nicaragua—

and emerged unscathed; and he *bluffed* and survived—even when threatening the murderous Pancho Villa. He survived all this, and much more, and died a commonplace, quiet death—obscure and forgotten.

Whatever deity had been assigned to watch over him beginning in 1909, it deserted him forty years later.

Tracy Custer Richardson first saw the light of day through a chinked window of a sod house in Broken Bow, Nebraska, on November 21, 1892. His parents moved to Lamar, Missouri, when Tracy was only a few months old, and Lamar became one of several of his "homes" and the one he returned to when his career reached its nadir after World War Two.

He attended Lamar public schools to the eighth grade, then took a job with the Prairie Oil and Gas Company on a pipeline project running from Morris, Oklahoma, to Baton Rouge, Louisiana, working as timekeeper, commissary clerk, and purchasing agent for the company. Louisiana, at the southern end of the pipeline, Tracy learned, was the debarkation point for all kinds of adventuresome expeditions into Central America, and in 1909 he parted company with the Prairie Oil job to make what he called "a trip around the tropics."

On his abrupt little "Personal History" sheet, Tracy speaks of "Joining the Nicaraguan revolutionary army," and "remaining in Nicaragua" through 1909-1910, but this scarcely tells the story of his debut as a soldier of fortune. One Richardson exploit in that Central American country is so fantastic it smacks of myth—but is true, nonetheless.

After "joining the Nicaraguan revolutionary army" in 1909—a ragtag crew of rebels opposed to the dictatorship of Jose Santos Zelaya—Tracy rode with the rebel General Luis Mena toward the city of Managua and found himself scouting far ahead of his column to avoid the smothering clouds of dust raised by Mena's horsemen. Without realizing it, the teen-aged *Americano* rode into the city (population then of about 20,000), and found himself surrounded by a squad of federal soldiers.

Richardson, with the first of what would become a legendary series of bluffs, said authoritatively, "I am a messenger from the commander of the revolution to your commanding general. Take me to him." Nonplussed, the *federales* escorted the gritty "messenger" to the federal garrison's commander. Once there, Richardson's stone-faced *sang-froid* stayed with him. Tracy boomed his threat to the incredulous *jefe*: "General Luis Mena has sent me to give you a chance for your life. Managua is surrounded at this minute. We outnumber you ten to one."

The Managua commander considered the situation for a moment, mentally weighing what the brash young man before him had said and, no doubt, concluding that *no one* would be stupid enough to ride into Managua with such a message if it were not true. Then, to Tracy's barely-concealed amazement, the *jefe* surrendered his forces to the American "messenger" from General Mena.

Later, in another recorded feat of the Nicaraguan revolt, Tracy and another man were credited with "wiping out a Nicaraguan federal regiment with two machine-guns mounted behind sandbags concealed with shrubbery."

The second and third flags in Tracy's new career came equally as quickly. Briefly he joined a revolutionary band in Venezuela early in 1911, fighting against the tyrannic government of Juan Vicente Gomez; then, given $600 in gold by "recruiters" for the already-famous banana republic filibuster, General Lee Christmas, Tracy joined Christmas' forces in the fever jungles of Honduras.

Lee Christmas of New Orleans might be called Tracy Richardson's spiritual and philosophic godfather. Born on a plantation on the Amite River, Livingston Parish, Louisiana, in 1863, Christmas' early career was spent mundanely as a locomotive engineer before he found the wars, adventure, renown, and gold of the Central American tinder-box republics to his liking. Before his illustrious career ended in his death in 1924 (from a variety of jungle disease called "tropic spruce" which caused an incurable anemia), Christmas had served as general in the armies of five Central American countries. He had, in addition, earned a reputation as rebel leader and jungle fighter second only to that of the great American filibuster-soldier William Walker, who died before a Nicaraguan firing-squad in 1860.

(Richard Harding Davis, the dashing newspaper correspondent and author who came to know many of the professional mercenary soldiers of his day, used Lee Christmas as the model for the hero "Clay" in the famous Davis novel, *Soldier of Fortune*.)

Tracy's growing prowess with a machine-gun (he once said, "It's a curious thing the way a machine-gun takes hold of you if you're a natural-born machine-gunner") earned him a colonelcy under Lee Christmas and he fought valiantly in the Honduran Bonilla revolt with the great New Orleans soldier.

Another soldier of fortune Tracy met with Christmas' army would become a life-long friend. This was Sam Dreben, "the Fighting Jew." Dreben, born in Russia in about 1878, came to the United States at the age of 20 where he enlisted for duty in the Philippine Insurrection that followed the Spanish-American War. Afterward, Dreben served in China, during the relief of Peking in the Boxer Rebellion of 1900, then had drifted back to the United States, seeking adventure as an irregular soldier—and finding it with the redoubtable Lee Christmas in Honduras.

After the Bonilla Revolt ended, Tracy and Sam Dreben were in New Orleans planning a gun-running expedition to Venezuela when emissaries of anti-Madero forces in Mexico invited the two adventurers to carry their business enterprises into the northern part of that country. Tracy and Sam sold their services for $500 in gold a month to the two *caudillos*, Gen. Ynez Salazar and Gen. Emiliano Campa, who had just captured the city of Juarez, across the Rio Grande from El Paso, Texas. The two *Americanos* joined Salazar's column (soon to ally with Pascual Orozco) outside Juarez and took part in a series of obscure skirmishes—at places such as Rellano Jiminez, Pedricena, Hacienda de la Refugio, and Villa Lopez.

For *gringos*, even such capable machine-gunning ones as Tracy Richardson and Sam Dreben, life in any of the various Mexican rebel "armies" was a constant struggle to stay alive—not only on the battlefield, but in camp in times of relative quiet. The volatile Mexican *generales*, ever-suspicious that the Americans would decamp to an opposing army on the signal of the tinkling of gold coins, frequently exploded in anger at the slightest provocation. For some Americans such a situation ended in a final tableau before a hastily summoned firing squad.

Gen. Campa was this very sort of short, smoldering-fused *jefe* and for some unknown reason conceived an intense dislike and distrust for three *gringos* in his ranks—Tracy, Sam Dreben, and a tall, baby-faced adventurer named Jack Zimmerman. Once, during the Chihuahua campaigning, Campa lined the three men up against an adobe wall, threatening to have his execution squad open fire. In true story-book style, however, the three American *soldados* were reprieved at the last moment—with a warning from Campa that the next parade before the wall would be the last.

Tracy Richardson is often mentioned as an "American Villista,"

Tracy Richardson as a Captain in the Canadian Expeditionary Force during WWI (from ***Liberty Magazine****, Oct. 10, 1925)*

but in truth he never fought *for* the famous Pancho. There exists one tale, possibly apocryphal, possibly true, that Villa once placed a $10,000 ransom on Tracy's head—perhaps as a theatrical gesture by Villa to show his consuming hatred for any man, Mexican or American, who rode with an opposition camp. In any case, so the story goes, Tracy ran into Villa and Pancho's sinister bodyguard Rodolfo Fierro in an El Paso saloon in 1912. Tracy, perhaps utilizing the bluff technique he had honed to a fine edge in Nicaragua, or perhaps simply overendowed with guts (something he proved time and time again), is supposed to have had a heated conversation with Villa on the matter of the $10,000 bounty and, with Fierro looking grimly on, forced the unarmed Pancho to back down and apologize for the "inconvenience" he had caused.

In 1914, Tracy left the Mexican border to join the forces of the diminutive Kansas game-cock, Gen. Frederick Funston, when American troops landed at Vera Cruz. Tracy served briefly with Funston as an intelligence officer—his inside knowledge of revolutionary Mexico coming in quite handy—with the rank of "Acting Captain" and the pay to go with it.

At the age of 22, the Lamar, Missouri, fighter had matured beyond his tender years. He was a lean, sun-baked six-footer with a perpetual squint in his eyes from staring into tropical suns, a well-trimmed dark moustache, prominent nose, close-cropped sandy hair—if not exactly handsome, at least looking every inch the professional soldier-adventurer.

Between Mexico and Tracy's journey to Canada, there is a short, mysterious chapter in his career in which he served, perhaps only a few weeks, as a Customs Collector in Guatemala. It is believed the job came as a reward for his participation in a coup or revolt in that country. Whatever the case, the Great War in Europe, breaking out in August 1914, with the sythe-like sweep of the Kaiser's soldiers into neutral Belgium, gave Tracy the opportunity to shake the jungle mud from his boots. A month after the European War began, he had made his way to Canada (his own country, which he had but little seen in the previous five years, would not participate in the War for another three years), anxious to get to the fight.

For the first phase of his World War service, Tracy chose one of Canada's most illustrious units, Princess Patricia's Canadian Light Infantry Regiment, which welcomed him as a seasoned machine-gunner, a commodity soon to be badly needed on the Western Front of France. During the short training period in Canada,

Tracy met a few other Americans eager to get into the fighting, among them a tall and immensely likeable fellow named Frederick Faust, and called "Heinie"—in a friendly way, of-course. Faust, who had a heart flutter that would soon wash him out of any chance for active service in France, also had a flair for writing and not too many years thence would become famous under the most renowned of his many pen-names, "Max Brand."

The training period ended, Tracy joined the Princess Pats in the freezing trenches of Belgium in January 1915. He fought bravely in the bloody attrition battles of St. Elois and Vimy Ridge, then took a serious series of wounds on May 4, 1915, during the Second Battle of Ypres.

Convalescing in a British hospital behind the lines at Rouen, Tracy was interviewed by a New York *Times* reporter whose story subsequently received the headline, "The 'Machine-gun Man of the Princess Pats'." The report, published in the *Times* on October 31, 1915, said: "Down in El Paso, in Vera Cruz, at Del Rio, at Nogales, in Central America, where Tracy's name was a household word, his friends had heard that he was dead; that he had 'gone to glory,' as one of them put it, fighting to the last in the very face of a vicious German assault. Then came the news from Tracy himself that he was still very much alive, although 'considerably holed up,' as he referred to the three wounds from which he was recovering."

The *Times* quoted Tracy as saying, "I was wounded in the back early in the morning [of May 4, 1915] by a piece of shell which struck me between the shoulders and plowed down my back and lodged just over my hip bone, where it still remains. About noon, I caught a piece of shell through the right leg. By this time we had only one man on the gun who was unwounded. At five o'clock the Germans scored a direct hit on our gun with a six-inch shell, and the gun was gone, and I had another wound in the right leg."

Of his convalescence, Tracy was quoted as saying, "I was sent to a hospital at Rouen where they kept me for 23 days, and then sent me over here to England, where the folks talk 'American' and where they are all good to you. I have been here ever since, and the day is drawing near for my return to the front.

"I am pretty well shot up," he continued, "but not a 'goner' by a long shot. They may order me before a medical board when I get back to Flanders, and should they rule me out of action for good, I'll come back to Texas and get ready perhaps for Mexico. Who can tell? From the little I hear, things seem to be up and doing in

Mexico and maybe the bubble will 'bust' yet. Well, this is enough for one time. Remember me to the fellows in El Paso."

As it turned out, the medical board felt Tracy still had some life in him and he was permitted to return to service, this time receiving a commission in the 97th Batallion, Canadian Expeditionary Force—called, because of the sizable number of Americans in it, the "Yank Battalion." Later, Tracy transferred to the British Royal Naval Air Service, received flight training at Vendome, Fance, and flew patrols over the North Sea. He also served as instructor in pursuit flying and combat at Cranwell, England, until 1918 when he transferred to the American Army Signal Corps as a pilot. He attended an American flying school at Issoudun, France; spent some time in the U.S., commanding an Aerial Gunnery School at Selfridge Field, Mount Clemens, Michigan; and ended the war commanding the Aerial Gunnery School at St. Jean De Monte, France.

And, sandwiched between all this activity, Tracy obtained a short leave of absence before the war ended to go to London where he received a certificate in mining based on his studies begun in 1915 when hospitalized and recovering from his Ypres wounds at Manchester, England.

From the end of the Great War until his death, Tracy's life was a peripatetic one—and astoundingly calm, though, far-flung, for a man who spent nearly a decade behind a chattering machine-gun in trouble spots from Vera Cruz to France. After his discharge from the Army Air Corps in 1919, he prospected in Northern Canada; explored mining areas of the Patuca River region of Honduras; conducted an oil survey in Guatemala; surveyed the mahogany timber country in the state of Chiapas, Mexico; worked for the Burns Detective Agency in New Orleans; sold real estate in Florida and Washington, D.C.; worked as a police reporter for the Chicago *Herald-Examiner* and as a prohibition agent in New York City; managed a gold mine at Ixtapan del Oro, Mexico in 1930; worked on an oil-drilling rig at Tyler, Texas; and worked mines of various kinds in Spokane, Washington, and Cripple Creek, Colorado.

Tracy's post-war career included at least three incidents in which he was arrested and jailed on various charges—once for "rudely displaying and flourishing a deadly weapon," again for mail fraud, and a third time for murder. He was cleared of all three crimes. The murder charge came about in 1922 when he shot and killed a man named John Murphy in New Orleans. Tracy's explanation was simple: he said he killed Murphy "after the man had attacked me and twice wounded me." The case was presented to a New Orleans Gand Jury which returned a "no-bill" and agreed that Tracy had killed in self-defense and at the time of the incident, had been working as a special officer and thus had a permit to carry a pistol.

In 1933, the veteran campaigner stayed a year in Albuquerque, working in various unimportant mining jobs. The times were apparently difficult for him and Tracy wrote to his old friend from the Princess Pats, "Heinie" Faust (by now world-famous as "Max Brand," author of a zillion words of western fiction), asking for a loan of $250. Faust came through and Tracy moved back to New Orleans where he eked out a living at various jobs—among them writing for pulp magazines.

In 1941, he returned to active service, first as intelligence officer in the Eastern Procurement District, later as air inspector and base commander with the Second Air Force in Colorado. After a short stint of duty in the Aleutian Islands, he was discharged from the Army as a lieutenant colonel on January 13, 1946.

Tracy's skein was now quickly running out. The two men he held in warmest admiration were dead. Lee Christmas succumbed to his jungle fever anemia on January 21, 1924; the "Fighting Jew," Sam Dreben, collapsed in a doctor's office in Hollywood, California, on March 15, 1925—dead at the age of 47, after compiling a career in World War One that surpassed that of Tracy himself. Dreben had earned a Distinguished Service Cross in October 1918, for combat at St. Etienne, and returned home with the DSC, Medaille Militaire, Croix de Guerre with palms, and a tunic-full of other medals. Now he, too, had gone.

Tracy, veteran of five or six wars, untold battles, untold honors from at least seven nations, and 16 wounds as badges of special honor, spent his last three years of life hawking household appliances door to door in Missouri—close by his home town of Lamar.

He died on April 22, 1949, in Springfield, Missouri, virtually forgotten. But years earlier, the great war correspondent Richard Harding Davis—who knew Tracy in Mexico and in France—said of the bold machine-gunner: "Tracy Richardson has lived more soldier of fortune tales than I could ever write." It was not, but could have been, chiseled on the Richardson tombstone, right under the timeworn message—so appropriate for one who sought war all his life—"Rest in Peace."

Sources:

- "He Died in Bed," *Everyday Magazine,* St. Louis *Post Dispatch,* May 8, 1959.
- Kansas City (Missouri) *Journal-Post*, February 27, 1938.
- Lester D. Langley, *The Banana Wars: An Inner History of of American Empiring, 1900-1934* (1983).
- "Machine-Gunner of the Princess Pats," New York *Times*, October 31, 1915.
- "A Soldier of Fortune's Story," *Liberty Magazine*, October-December 1925.

Richardson, working his weapon, a French-made Hotchkiss, firing 8mm cartridges from metal strips carrying 30 rounds each. This photo taken during the Bonilla revolt in Honduras in 1910 (from ***Liberty Magazine****, Oct. 10, 1925)*

Frank Luke

Arizona Balloon-Buster

In telling the story of Frank Luke you have to deal first with the statistics on his career—numbers so astonishing they tend to overshadow the man.

Luke wore the uniform of the United States Air Service from September 25, 1917, until September 29, 1918. Of those 369 days, he spent six weeks on the Western Front and, of that time, 17 days in actual combat situations. Of the 17 days of combat patrols, his total air time was about 30 hours.

In this period, Luke shot down a minimum of 15 German observation balloons and four enemy planes. One of his exploits occurred on September 18, 1918, when he destroyed three planes and two balloons in 20 minutes.

Some lists credit Luke with a total of 21 balloons and planes and his C.O., Major Harold Hartney, said the final tally should have been at least 28. But 18 or 21 victories, the most reasonable range, Luke became the second-ranking American Ace of the war, behind Eddie Rickenbacker of the 94th "Hat in the Ring" squadron.

To get a mental image of Frank Luke, one might recall the stereotypical soldiers of the war movies, especially those grade-B and below. There was always a "Peck's Bad Boy" type among them: young, handsome, sullen, two-fisted, grudge carrying, undisciplined; capable of egotistical outbursts that irritated everyone around him, standing on the brink of court martial, ostracized by his barrack mates, seemingly bent on winning the war single-handedly. Often this character was blonde with steely blue eyes.

In the movies such a figure was an obvious figment of a writer's imagination, but such a figure was Frank Luke inside and out. For all we know, in fact, Luke may have been the original pattern of the brash young Yank of the war movies and maybe the original inspiration for the phrase the French used in two world wars: *"Tout les Americans sont fous!"*—All Americans are crazy!

Nearly everyone who knew Luke (and quite a number who didn't) tried to explain him. Major Harold Hartney, Luke's commander in the 27th squadron and later commander of the entire First Pursuit Group in France, had perhaps the best grasp of the character of the wild fighter from Phoenix. Hartney (a

Luke as a newly commissioned 2nd. Lt. in the U.S. Air Service, January 1918 (Arizona Historical Society, Tucson)

Canadian) saw Luke as a product of the wild and wooly American West, a still untamed territorial Arizona. He wrote of Luke as a failure as a mixer and joiner, as shy and self-conscious but an occasional braggart, a man who questioned authority openly and openly defied it if it didn't mesh with his own ideas and plans. Luke was a loner, Hartney said, and had few close friends.

In the Western territories of America, there was nothing strange about such a man as this.

As to the incredible chances he took, his flight leader, Jerry Vasconcelles said: "Luke has no imagination. He can't imagine anything happening to him. He thinks he's invincible."

Frank Luke Jr. was one of nine children of Frank Luke, a German immigrant from Dalhausen who first settled in Brooklyn, then moved to Phoenix in 1880. Young Frank graduated from high school in 1916, took a job in a copper mine at Ajo, Arizona, and through the urging of his sister Eva, a nurse with the Red Cross in Europe, enlisted in the Aviation Section of the U.S. Signal Corps on September 25, 1917.

Frank had the routine training at the School of Military Aeronautics in Austin, Texas, and more at Rockwell Field in San Diego. He received his commission as a 2nd Lieutenant on January 23, 1918, and in March shipped to France. He had his aerial gunnery training at Cazeaus, learned to fly Nieuports, Salmsons and Spads, and was posted to the 27th Aero Squadron of the First Pursuit Group in July. It would be a month before he would fly his first patrol.

The 27th had entered the rolls on June 23, 1917, and by the end of the year, Maj. Harold E. Hartney had taken over its command. It was one of four squadrons making up the First Pursuit Group: the 94th, 95th, 147th and 27th. A Private Dunkel came up with a picture from a stateside magazine which depicted an eagle swooping out of the morning sun and this was selected as the 27th's fuselage emblem.

By the time Luke and another replacement named Joseph Fritz Wehner joined the squadron in July 1918, it was located at Saints, a village about 25 miles south of Chateau-Thierry in the old Aisne-Marne salient. The airdrome there was a typical affair—an L-shaped field with canvas hangars, miscellaneous ramshackle out-buildings of corrugated tin roofs and wood frames, smoke spiraling up from the chimney of the cookshack.

The 27th flew the Spad 13 (the acronym "Spad" taken from the

Frank Luke, Jr., with his battered Spad 13, one of several he flew in his six-week career on the Western Front of France in WWI (Author's files)

manufacturer, the "Societe Pour L'Aviation et ses Derives"), a machine with a 26′-6″ wingspan, a little over 20 feet in length, weighing 1,862 pounds. It was equipped with a 220 horsepower Hispano-Suiza ("Hisso") engine which gave the plane a maximum speed of 139 mph. The Spad 13 had a ceiling of 21,800 feet and a combat range of 185 miles. It was armed with twin 7.65 mm Vickers machine-guns synchronized to fire through the propeller arc.

The pattern for Frank Luke's behavior in the 27th squadron was established on his first combat patrol. It took place on August 16, 1918, when Hartney led a flight of 12 planes of the First Pursuit Group out of the airdrome at Coincy. They were to fly at 9,000 feet to protect a Salmson photography plane taking pictures along the enemy trenches. Hartney developed engine trouble after a time and flew home with an unidentified German plane on his tail most of the way. Luke came in shortly after and told Hartney he had "shot down an e.a. near Soissons." In his report, Luke wrote: "I do not know the exact location as this being my first combat did not notice closely but know that it was some distance within German territory for Archie followed me for about 10 minutes on my way back." ("Archie" being slang for enemy anti-aircraft ground fire.) He told Hartney: "I never pulled the triggers until I had my gun right in that baby's cockpit. And I didn't leave him until he hit the ground and rolled over on his back, with me not more than 200 feet in the air."

Luke never received confirmation for this first claim, although Hartney recorded in his post-war memoirs: "He was not lying and I know it."

After that August 16 incident, Luke began pecking out confirmation letters with one finger on a borrowed typewriter, leaving blanks to be filled in and signed by eyewitnesses. He took them with him on his patrols thereafter.

How Luke became interested in enemy observation balloons is a matter of some dispute. Hartney, who assumed command of the Group on August 21, told the story of taking a walk with Luke in the vicinity of Fere-en Tardenois, soon joining a group of American infantrymen watching a German plane pouring incendiary bullets into an American balloon swaying on its cables nearby. The balloon exploded in a gush of flame, the observers leaping from their baskets as the German Albatross blithely turned toward his lines. Hartney believed this sight planted a seed: "I am positive that on that homeward trip, Luke laid out his future course and made his plans to become our most spectacular flier and world's greatest strafer of enemy balloons."

Another story is that Luke paid occasional visits to the French Spad 3 squadron—"the Storks"—whose airdrome was not far from the 27th's at Saints. There, the story goes, he overheard France's bravest and most decorated fliers say they would rather face two German planes than one German observation balloon, so dangerous was this "sport."

Arch Whitehouse, prolific writer on WWI aviation, had a simpler—and quite possibly truer—opinion. Whitehouse has written that Luke decided to hunt balloons because he knew if he shot one down there would be no question of his getting credit for it. A balloon victory was a very visible thing.

That they were a dangerous prey is beyond question. The typical German *drachen* ("dragon") or kite balloon was made of rubberized silk, upwards of 200 feet in length, hanging in the sky two miles or so behind their lines, usually at about 2,000 feet. They were anchored to heavy trucks on the ground by steel cables which were played out or reeled in by high-speed winches. The bags were inflated with highly-flammable hydrogen gas and were thus vulnerable, or so it seemed, to incendiary bullets. The observers swung in a basket beneath the balloon, watching troop movements through their field glasses and telescopes—capable of seeing 10 miles distance into the opposite lines—and equipped with air-to-ground telephones to report their sightings, and enormous parachutes by which they could float to the ground if under attack.

Both sides, for obvious reasons, highly prized their "obs" and the German *drachen* were protected by a circle of quick-firing anti-aircraft guns, teams of ground machine-gunners, and fighter planes circling above. One dreaded weapon used by the Germans to ward off attack on their balloons was the "flaming onion," a shell that exploded into a shower of fireballs that could burn the doped fabric off an airplane.

The dangers in fighting these unlovely beasts were also obvious: the balloon strafer had to fly close to them to get his burst of incendiary ammunition into the target; he ran the danger of flying into the long, looping cables swaying in the wind; he had to endure the rain of fire from ground batteries below and enemy planes guarding their *drachen* from above.

Also, incendiary bullets did not always work—they often seemed to choke out in passing through the bag envelope, failing to

Luke and the LVG he shot down on Sept. 18, 1918, the day Fritz Wehner, his closest friend, was killed. This was Luke's fifth victory—two balloons and three planes—scored on that day alone. (Author's files)

ignite it. A few pilots, such as Norman Prince of the Spad 124 squadron, tried Le Prieur rockets mounted on a brace between the wings and fired electrically from the cockpit. These "Fourth of July" type rockets were scary; so erratic they could do a 360-degree circle in the air and home in on their owner.

On top of all this, the explosion of the hydrogen gas created a tremendous vacuum for a second or so and the pilot flying too close ran the danger of being sucked toward the flames, or at least having his machine severely buffeted in the wake of the heat and exploding gas.

Luke won his first confirmed victory—a balloon—on September 12, flying an early morning patrol with seven other planes during the St. Mihiel offensive. He had his confirmation forms with him when he spotted the *drachen* at Marieville and destroyed it after three passes, each within a few yards of the bag. The final pass was made as the balloon had neared the ground, the frantic winch operators reeling it in. Luke's Vickers jammed momentarily, but he cleared the faulty shell and had turned to squeeze off a final burst when the balloon flamed up and dropped on the winch crew, killing several men. Luke landed at an American balloon hangar near the enemy lines and found two eyewitnesses to his exploit. He got his confirmation chits signed and delivered them to the 27th's new C.O., Capt. Alfred Grant.

Two days later, Luke ran his score up two notches. He joined a 9:30 patrol and split off from his comrades at Boinville, diving at a German *drachen* a frustrating six times at close range, clearing two gun stoppages in between. After about 75 rounds, the balloon deflated and sank to the ground "in a very flabby condition," Luke reported. He strafed the ground crew and gun battery for good measure, then returned to the 27th airdrome to await the afternoon sortie. This commenced at 2:30 and he flew with Fritz Wehner, his only real friend in the squadron. The two dropped out of formation at Buzy and with Wehner flying guard, Luke attacked his second balloon of the day, bringing it down in flames. Eight Fokkers dropped out of the sky in the middle of the balloon attack, but Wehner drove through the enemy formation, miraculously scattering it.

Joseph Fritz Wehner, born in Boston of German immigrant parents, had suffered for his origins. Secret Service men questioned him several times in the course of his flying training, this in a time of anti-German hysteria in the U.S. when sauerkraut became known for a time as "Liberty cabbage," and people kicked dachshunds on the street. Ironically, Wehner teamed up with another whose father was German-born and the two men seemed to find some friendship in one another they found missing amongst their companions in the 27th.

(Perhaps even more ironic, the premier American Ace of the war, Eddie Rickenbacker, was of German parentage, as was Jimmy Meissner of the 94th squadron and Medal of Honor winner Harold Coettler who died flying supplies to the Lost Battalion. But then even the Commander-in-Chief of the American Expeditionary Force, John Joseph Pershing's family name was originally Pfoershing in their homeland of Alsace.)

One of Luke's greatest exploits took place during the two days following his double balloon victory. He had talked to Grant and Hartney of a plan to fly a mission at dusk near Boinville where two balloons had now replaced the one deflated on the 14th. Luke was delegated to relate his plan directly to Gen. Billy Mitchell, then paying a visit to the 27th's billet. "Wehner and I are going to try out our dusk stuff at Boinville," Luke told Mitchell and his staff member, "and if you gentlemen will come back here at just about dusk, Major Hartney will give you the exact time when they are going to burn."

The next morning, September 15, Luke flew two patrols with the 27th and couldn't resist dropping out of formation at Boinville and shooting down both balloons as the other members of the flight served as his unwitting escort, fighting off enemy Fokkers that swooped down on them. When news of the Boinville caper reached Mitchell, the USAS chief called his First Pursuit Group commander: "Hartney, the French got your two balloons at Boinville, so you won't be able to stage that show tonight, will you?" Hartney informed Mitchell that it was not the French but Frank Luke who burned the balloons and that Luke now wanted the show to go on, substituting two others, one northwest of Verdun and the other near Chaumont. Hartney told Mitchell to be at the 27th drome at six and not to be late. The first balloon was scheduled to burn at 6:58 and there would be a grandstand seat waiting.

Mitchell and his aides arrived in the General's Benz (he disliked the Germans but loved their cars, Hartney said), and after drinking some coffee, the party sauntered over to the brow of a nearby hill as darkness fell and only the distant rumble of artillery could be heard. Off in the distance toward Verdun, in the gathering evening mist, the German *drachen* swayed in the wind.

At precisely 6:58, a tongue of flame shot into the sky at Spincourt, followed by a huge burst of flame. "By God! There she goes!" the normally poised Mitchell shouted, dancing a jig in his excitement. This was Wehner's work. A few minutes later, at Bois d'Hingry, a second orange flash lit the sky for a second. Luke had his sixth victory.

The runway was lighted and soon Luke taxied up to a stop, Wehner coming behind a few minutes later, both making perfect landings, rolling up directly in front of Hartney, Mitchell and crowd that had gathered. Even Eddie Rickenbacker was there, thumping Luke and Wehner on the back. Mitchell took his swagger-stick and pulled chunks of wing cover off Wehner's machine—each Spad had at least 50 bullet holes in it and both were taken off service.

The "show" on the 15th being so successful, Luke presented a plan to Hartney for another dusk attack the next day. The targets were three balloons southeast of Verdun. Plenty of protection was to be afforded and once again Mitchell and his entourage were to be witnesses. Luke and Wehner took off at 6:45 and simultaneously three echelons of the 27th departed from Mount Sec, Verdun and Rembercourt.

At 7:05 the sky glowed red for an instant over Romagne as the two strafers hit the *drachen* as it was being winched in and swung less than 50 feet off the ground. The observer was burned to death as the flaming bag fell on him. Wehner took off then toward the Meuse river, flew back toward Verdun again and at near Mangiennes took the second balloon down with a single incendiary burst at 7:21 and in a furious hail of ground fire. Luke, meantime, burned his second balloon near Reville at 7:35.

Mitchell, standing with Hartney at the Rembercourt airdrome, shook his head: "Harold, it is the most amazing thing I have ever seen."

Fritz Wehner was killed two days later while on a balloon mission with Luke. The two had gone up at four that afternoon and climbed to 7,000 feet over St. Mihiel. Luke spotted a bag over a tiny spot on the map named Labeauville. Both climbed to some cloud cover, Luke looked behind him to find Wehner in protective position, then dived for the first *drachen.* Close on it, he fired a sustained burst and saw the top seam open, a flash of orange fire

Statue of Luke by sculptor Roy Noble Burnham, unveiled on Armistice Day, 1930. The pedestal contains the names of Arizona's sons who died in WWI. The statue is located on the Capitol grounds, Phoenix. (Arizona Historical Society, Tucson)

and a gush of burning hydrogen as the bag disintegrated, scattering flaming pieces of fabric to the ground. The second balloon swung lower and Luke reached it in a few minutes, firing a solid incendiary burst into it as "Archie" fire boomed about his Spad. The bag exploded with a muffled "whoomp" as Luke climbed to look for Wehner. His tail man was busily engaged with six Fokkers that had dropped from a high altitude too late to prevent Luke's handiwork but determined that the two would not return home.

Luke managed to take one of the D-7s off Wehner's tail, the twin Vickers pouring a stream of bullets head-on into the enemy machine; it spun down under Luke's landing gear, twisted once, spewing a black column of smoke, and spun toward the ground. Now Wehner's Spad had disappeared and Luke banked toward a second D-7, firing a short, lucky burst broadside that found its mark, the Fokker spinning out of control.

With the remaining four enemy planes milling around the sky, and with Wehner nowhere in sight, Luke flew low toward his lines. Near Verdun, he spotted several French Spads harassing a German LVG observation plane which had wandered out from its lines. Luke swerved toward it, bore down on it and fired, breaking the LVG up in the air.

By the time Luke landed at Rembercourt, his tank was bone dry.

A private in the 42nd (Rainbow) Division was an eyewitness to Luke's work on the LVG and reported the German machine had three Frenchmen "toying with it" when Luke came out of nowhere "like a rocket, streaked past the French and closed on the enemy as if he would ram it."

The day's work that September 18 was two enemy balloons and three planes in the space of about 20 minutes, bringing Luke's total to 13 in the seven days since his first balloon at Marieville. But more importantly, the day ended with Fritz Wehner dead, shot down in the midst of the six-Fokker attack.

Luke learned of Wehner's death some hours after he landed at Rembercourt. The news so depressed him that Hartney insisted he take a leave in Paris. Before they departed, Luke said, "Major, I'm glad it wasn't me. My mother doesn't even know I'm on the front yet."

He wrote a single letter from the capital, to his mother: "I have not written for some days now on account of being so busy, as no doubt you have already heard. This is only a line to let you know that I am o.k. Now, Mother, remember that I have passed the dangerous stage of being a new hand at the game, so don't worry, for I know how to take care of myself. Love to all, Frank."

After a week in Paris, Luke returned to the 27th airdrome at Rembercourt and flew a patrol on September 26 with a new partner, Lt. Ivan A. Roberts of South Lee, Mass. Luke got his 14th confirmed victory—a Fokker—but Roberts was killed. From now on, Luke flew alone.

Every pilot in the 27th had taken a crack at a pesky balloon over Batheville, and Captain Grant and Major Hartney had discussed letting Luke take a lone wolf patrol to bring it down. No decision on it had been reached, however, when on the afternoon of September 28, Luke took the matter into his own hands. He flew out at noon from Rembercourt and found the balloon, low on the ground and apparently in the act of being winched up. He burned it "in its nest," the strafer's term for less than 100 feet off the ground.

The next day, Luke flew his last sortie.

Three new balloons had been sited by the Germans, again in the vicinity of Verdun, and Luke begged Grant to let him go up alone against them. Grant refused, informing Luke that he was grounded for the unauthorized flight to Batheville. The Arizonan went over Grant's head directly to Major Hartney. Hartney knew nothing of Grant's grounding order, told Luke he could make the run, but not before sundown at 5:22.

Luke climbed into the Spad cockpit and began revving the engine 16 minutes early. He checked the Vickers belts and block, the hydraulic levels in the Constantinesco interruptor gear. Hartney chewed him out for attempting to leave early and left Luke chuckling in the Spad "office"—the only time, Hartney said, he ever saw Luke laughing out loud. Finally, at precisely 5:22, Luke taxied the Spad out and took off toward the Meuse and the village of Dun. He passed over the 7th American Balloon Company at Souilly and dropped a note. "Watch those three balloons on the Meuse. Luke."

What happened after that is a matter of varied testimony, the piecing together of the record from military ground observers and civilian villagers at Liney, Briere Farm, Milley, and Marveaus, along Luke's route. He flew along toward Dun at about 9,000 feet, swooped down on the first bag, levelled off and fired both Vickers broadside into the balloon which went up in a gush of flame on the first pass. Eight Fokker D-7s fell on his tail in an instant and there is some evidence that his Spad took some damaging machine gun slugs. He dove and flew low for a time and the Fokkers dispersed, apparently certain they had downed him. Luke emerged from low clouds at Briere Farm, fired the second balloon as it was being winched to the truck below, then veered off again for the village of Milley, another town on the Meuse river. Eyewitnesses said the American's Spad flew erratically, fluttered and hesitated. Luke, in all likelihood had been wounded.

He bore down on the third balloon at Milley and poured incendiary fire into it. It seemed to deflate but did not explode as it settled to the ground a little—then blew forth a golden flash of exploding gas.

Villagers at nearby Murveaux said the American machine did not make an effort to veer away from the explosion and some said the flaming fabric from the bag actually hit the Spad as it lumbered on toward their town. Luke's Spad barely missed the town church steeple, but he sideslipped to a nearby meadow and landed.

He was wounded and climbed painfully down from the cockpit, sat a few seconds on the trailing edge of the wing, back against the fuselage, then slipped to the ground and headed for a nearby stream. He had limped along nearly 50 yards, bathed his wound and drank at the stream, when a German infantry patrol emerged from the woods, heading for the Spad. Luke stumbled back to his plane, drew his service revolver and began firing. He was shot dead.

The Germans stripped off his shoes and leggings and took his wallet but inexplicably left his Elgin watch on his wrist. Murveaux villagers buried him near where he fell.

Frank Luke is the second-ranking American Ace of World War I, behind Captain Eddie Rickenbacker (with 26 victories, five of which were balloons) and just ahead of Raoul Lufbery (with 17). Among balloon aces of the war, Luke ranks 8th. Ahead of him among all-nations' aces are Lt. Michael Coiffard of France (28 balloons and six planes), Maj. Willy Coppens of Belgium (26 and 10), Capt. Maurice Coyeu of France (20 and 15), Oberlieutenant Heinrich Gontermann of Germany (18 and 21), Oblt. Fritz von Roth of Germany (17 and 11), Capt. A. W. Beauchamp-Proctor of South Africa (16 and 28), and Lt. Claude M. Haegelin of France (14 and 8).

Luke was awarded America's highest honor for combat valor, the Medal of Honor, on April 14, 1919. Eddie Rickenbacker, whose Medal of Honor was presented him 12 years later, said of

Luke: "He was . . . in my opinion the greatest fighting pilot in the war."

Graves Registration found his unmarked grave after the war and Luke was reinterred in the U.S. Cemetery at Romagne. On his white cross are the words: Frank Luke, Jr., 2 Lt., 27th Aero Sqdn., Arizona, September 1918."

Sources:

- Norman S. Hall, *The Balloon-Buster: Frank Luke of Arizona* (1928).
- Quentin Reynolds, *They Fought for the the Sky* (1957).
- Eddie V. Rickenbacker, *Fighting the Flying Circus* (1919, 1965).
- Arch Whitehouse, *Decisive Air Battles of the First World War* (1963)
  " " *Heroes of the Sunlit Sky* (1967).

Luke's grave at the American Cemetery, Romagne, France (Author's files)

Robert E. Howard
of Cross Plains, Texas

Robert E. Howard

Conan in the Post Oaks

"I have spent most of my time in the hard, barren semi-waste lands of Western Texas," Robert Erwin Howard once wrote, "and since infancy my memory holds a continuous grinding round of crop failures—sandstorms—droughts—floods—hot winds that withered the corn—hailstorms that ripped the grain to pieces—late blizzards that froze the fruit in the bud—plagues of grasshoppers and boll weevils that stripped the cotton."

This autobiographical statement from the creator of "Conan the Barbarian" and innumerable other fantasies of life before the dawn of recorded history is a dourly revealing passage. Howards' brief life (1906-1936) was as dull, stunted and ugly as the Texas post oak country he called home and it is small wonder that as a writer he lost himself in ages and lands that never existed.

Born in Peaster, Texas, an only child of Dr. Isaac Mordecai Howard and Hester Jane Erwin, young Robert was shuttled around such boom-and-bust towns as Seminole, Bagwell, Burkett, Brownwood and Cross Plains. When he was old enough to work, he picked cotton, hauled garbage, branded yearlings and clerked. He managed to get a high school education and even took a couple of college courses. He also learned to type and take shorthand, tools useful to him in his growing ambition to write professionally.

He read voraciously, read everything he could get his hands on, and later wrote to friends about that strange stew of reading: Conan Doyle, Jack London, Mark Twain, Sax Rohmer (creator of the "Fu Manchu" mysteries), Jeffrey Farnol, Talbot Mundy, Harold Lamb, Rider Haggard, Kipling, Walter Scott, Arthur Machen, Poe, Ambrose Bierce, H. P. Lovecraft, Balzac and De Maupassant. He read poetry from John Masefield to the Benets, from Rupert Brooke to Baudelaire, from Bret Harte to Sappho.

He said he never read Bernard Shaw or Joseph Conrad and disliked H. L. Mencken, Theodore Dreiser, Sinclair Lewis, Sherwood Anderson and F. Scott Fitzgerald intensely. "I'd rather read Zane Grey the rest of my life," he said, not indicating if he felt this a fate worse than having to read Mencken and company or if he felt Zane Grey better than the others. Probably he meant the latter.

Out of all this reading and out of his understandable desire to escape the oppressing ennui of life in small-town northwest Texas (Cross Plains, where he and his family finally settled, is in Callahan County and has a population today of about 1,500), he began creating his own fantasy worlds and writing about them.

"I have lived in the Southwest all my life," he would say, "yet most of my dreams are laid in cold, giant lands of icy wastes and gloomy skies, and of wild, wind-swept fens and wilderness over which sweep great sea-winds, and which are inhabited by shock-headed savages with light fierce eyes... Always I am the barbarian."

Howard wrote his first story at the age of nine. At 15, he later recalled, "having never seen a writer, a poet, a publisher, or a magazine editor, and having only the vaguest idea of procedure, I began working at the profession I had chosen."

By age 18 he had sold his first piece of fiction, beginning a non-stop 12-year career as contributor to the pulps, principally to a popular pulp (one which even today has an almost cult-collector following) called *Weird Tales*, a long-lived horror-fantasy magazine which could boast among its contributors such budding talents as Tennessee Williams, Mark Schorer, Ray Bradbury and August Derleth.

Howard soon became one of the most popular contributors to *Weird Tales*, vying for cover stories and choice inside space with the likes of H. P. Lovecraft, Clark Ashton Smith and Seabury Quinn—among the most popular writers of the horror-fantasy genre in the 1920-1940 era.

"Writing has always been a means to an end I hoped to achieve," Howard said in an autobiographical essay, adding with some pride, "To the best of my knowledge I am the first writer to be produced by a section of the country comprising a territory equal to that of the state of Connecticut...I was the first writer of the post oak country; my work's lack of merit cannot erase that fact."

That "lack of merit" may have been the opinion of literary scholars but not of the general run of readers in the era of the Great Depression when working people carried pulp magazines in their lunch pails and when every newsstand was bedecked with the garish covers of those ragged-edged magazines, the majority of which sold for a dime or 15 cents.

Beginning with that first *Weird Tales* story, "Spear and Fang," in the July 1925 issue (for which he received $16), Howard's output was steady and varied. He wrote some excellent horror tales, sports and western stories, and even some verse. (Two of his poems appeared in the 1933 edition of *Modern American Poetry.*) He wrote for such pulps as *Ghost Stories, Fight Stories, Oriental Stories, Argosy* and *Magic Carpet.*

In 1926 he earned $50 from his writing; by 1931, his income had risen to $1,500. The deepening depression dealt a blow to the pulp market and Howard's income dipped, as did everybody else's, but it rose again, reaching over $2,000 in 1935—a very respectable earning for that time.

Howard's chief claim to fame today is as creator of the sub-genre of the fantasy tale known in science fiction and fantasy circles as the "sword and sorcery" story. His 18 published tales about Conan of Cimmeria, the first of which appeared in *Weird Tales* in December 1932, were among the most popular fiction ever to appear in *Weird Tales.*

After his death, his Conan stories were collected in hard-cover books, and, more recently, in an on-going series of paperbacks (which include a number of "pastiches," stories allegedly made from Howard's notes, as well as wholly invented "new adventures" of the Cimmerian).

A group of Howard/Conan devotees began publishing critical studies of Howard's work and a giant book by a Howard authority, Glen Lord, *The Last Celt,* containing biographical and extensive bibliographical information, was published 40 years after Howard's death and is itself a collector's item today.

The connection between Howard and his Conan character is ironic. He created a number of memorable fictional heroes, nearly all better conceived than Conan: King Kull, who lived in an age when Atlantis was a savage wilderness; a dour Puritan named Solomon Kane who brawled his way through the jungles of Africa and other exotic places battering down blood-stained heathen idols and altars, armed only with a huge, iron-bound Bible; and Bran Mak Morn who "came of a race that was very old, which had spread over Western Europe in one vast Dark Empire, before the flood of Aryan conquest."

Even Howard's western characters, Buckner J. Grimes and Breckenridge Elkins, have their moments.

Conan, however, has survived when all the others are but dim memories of the Golden Age of Pulps.

The Conan stories are plotless devices enabling Howard to move his hero around primeval Europe, Asia and Africa, breaking bones and cleaving skulls in twain. He never wrote worse prose, demonstrated such a poverty of imagination and vocabulary, as when writing of Conan:

> The captain drew his knife and ran at him bellowing, but before he could strike, Conan gripped his wrist with a wrench that tore the arm clean of its socket. The captain bellowed like an ox in agony, and then rolled clear across the deck as he was hurled contemptuously from his attacker, ripped a heavy ax from the rail and wheeled cat-like to meet the rush. . . (From *Conan the Conqueror,* Lancer Books, 1967)

While the stories are unremarkable, the character of Conan is so compelling that it continues today in comic books, animated TV cartoons and in the lavish and successful films starring Arnold Schwarzenegger.

The number of Conan-inspired superheroes in fantasy fiction, comics and films is beyond count.

Just as he reached his peak of pulp popularity and productivity, Howard's various psychoses overtook him.

He had always had, despite the blood-letting in his fiction, a preternatural fear of death, a paranoiac's belief that his "enemies" were lurking in the bushes, and a thoroughly classic unnatural attachment to his parents, his mother in particular.

One of the dark facets of Howard's mind is revealed by the only professional writer Howard ever met in person. E. Hoffman Price, then beginning his career as a horror-fantasy author, drove down to Cross Plains from Pawhuska, Oklahoma, in 1934, for the purpose of meeting the great myth-maker of the post oaks whose stories Price had read in *Weird Tales* and admired.

Price, in a memoir of Howard he wrote later, saw the Texas writer as a friendly, salty, colorful—and volcanic—man, seething with conflicts and mental anguish. On a drive around the Cross Plains area, Howard told Price he had "a lot of enemies" and always carried a gun. Howard would even stop the car periodically when spotting some furtive movement in the brush along the road.

After his son's death, Dr. I. M. Howard (he was an M.D.) wrote a telling letter about Robert's strange attitude toward death. When Robert's dog, aged 12, fell ill and was dying, Robert packed a bag and moved to Brownwood, there calling home each day to check on the situation. When the dog died, Robert returned and never spoke of the animal again.

E. Hoffman Price also made this significant observation: "I had often got the impression that Robert was a parent to his parents; that while he could have done the gypsying which other authors permitted themselves, solicitude for his father and mother kept him fairly close to home."

This problem went very deep indeed. Early in 1935, Howard's mother underwent a serious operation in Temple, Texas, and never recovered her health. The illness, surgery and periodic relapses drained the family's meager finances. Mrs. Howard, in the year following her surgery, fell constantly weaker and Robert threatened several times to take his own life if she died.

On the morning of June 11, 1936, Howard asked the nurse in attendance if his mother would ever recognize him again. The answer was no. Howard walked away from the house to his car, pulled a .38 caliber Colt automatic from the glovebox, placed the barrel on his temple and blew his brains out.

His mother died the next day without regaining consciousness and with no knowledge of her son's suicide.

Robert E. Howard, as much or more than his creations, was a tailor-made cult hero, in the manner of a James Dean—young, lonely, driven, talented, reaching to the limits of hard-earned talents, cut off in the prime of his life and talent, unrealized and subject of endless speculation on what he "might have done."

Whatever the case for this speculation, he did carve a niche for a brief time as the pulp king of the post oaks and his name will be remembered as long as Conan's is remembered—and thus far, that is 57 years and counting.

Sources:

- Glenn Lord, *The Last Celt: A Bio-Bibliography of Robert E. Howard,* 1976.
- Leonard Sanders, "Author's Life Brief, Tragic," Fort Worth, Texas, *Star-Telegram,* March 2, 1969.
- *The Howard Collector,* 18 issues, 1961-1973, published by Glenn Lord, Pasadena, Texas.

*Faust's "Untamed" as it appeared as the cover story of the December 7, 1918, issue of **All-Story Weekly** (Author's files)*

Max Brand

Lorenzo of the Pulps

He was best known as Max Brand and he was one of the most prolific writers America has ever produced. It has been established that he published some 25 million words in a writing career of 27 years (1917-1944)—the equivalent of over 500 books. In addition, he was a man whose prodigious energy, talent, generosity, kindliness of character, artistic unhappiness and capacity for whiskey were legend in his own time.

He wrote and sold so much so often that one name staggered under the burden of his authorship, so he wrote under the names Frank Austin, George Owen Baxter, Lee Bolt, Walter C. Butler, George Challis, Peter Dawson, Martin Dexter, Evan Evans, John Frederick, Dennis Lawton, David Manning, Peter Henry Morland, Hugh Owen, Nicholas Silver, Henry Uriel and Frederick Frost.

Sometimes a pulp magazine would appear with three or four of these names in the table of contents and several of the *noms de plume* gained reputations distinct from each other, though all were the work of one man.

In the Golden Age of Pulps, when he was King, he wrote western fiction, Northland and South Sea romances, sports stories, animal stories, fantasy fiction, detective fiction, sea, air and war stories, religious and humorous stories, medical and historical stories.

Poetry was his first love and his last and he wrote that, too. His fiction he knocked out by the ream, punching his typewriter keyboard with stumpy index fingers, a machine-like process, done grudgingly. His poem he *composed*, quill pen on paper, taking his time and enjoying every minute of it.

Today he is still best known as Max Brand and for such western novels as *Silvertip, Fightin' Fool, South of the Rio Grande, The Border Kid, Flaming Irons, King of the Range, The Longhorn Feud, Singing Guns, Montana Rides!, Valley Vultures, Twenty Notches, The Jackson Trail, The Outlaw* and *Lucky Larribee,* to name a few. His most famous western, *Destry Rides Again*, has been made into several movies, a TV series and a David Merrick musical on Broadway, and *The Untamed* (his first novel) has been filmed at least twice.

And, had he written no westerns at all, he would still be remembered as the creator of Dr. Kildare.

In his lifetime he published two slim volumes of poetry—scarcely a ripple on the ocean of words that flowed from him. The books were especially distinctive in that they were his only works published under his true name—Frederick Faust.

The life and times of Frederick Schiller Faust—Max Brand—reads like one of his own fiction works, only less credible. There is hardly an ordinary fact about him. He was born in Seattle on May 29, 1892, and in his childhood, hard work, poverty and loneliness were constant companions. (How often he must have reflected on that fact 35 years later as he roamed his capacious villa in Florence, Italy, between writing assignments.)

By the time he was 13, both parents had died and young Faust eked out a living by working on fruit farms and ranches in California's San Joaquin Valley. Between the long hours of manual labor and attending school, he had also begun to write.

"I had written enough to know I wanted to write more," he once jokingly recalled, "and at about the same time a high sense of destiny overcame me once and for all."

Faust estimated he attended 19 schools up and down the Pacific coast before graduating from Modesto (California) High School in 1910. His troublesome childhood may have driven him inward and away from normal adolescent experiences, but it also drove him toward books and toward a yearning for knowledge.

In the fall of 1911, Faust managed miraculously to enter the University of California where he settled down to major in social sciences and to become a regular contributor of jokes, poems and fiction to the campus humor magazine *The Pelican*, and the literary *Occident*. In 1915, failing to graduate from U.C., Faust voyaged to Hawaii and landed a job as reporter on the Honolulu *Star-Bulletin* at $15 a week. During his brief stint on the paper, Faust covered the 77th birthday party given for Queen Liliuokalani and got to see the last of Hawaii's monarchs up close.

The World War was on his mind from its beginning in the summer of 1914, and after a few months in Hawaii, he took ship to Vancouver, B.C., and enlisted in the Canadian Army, hoping to see duty on the Western Front in France.

In Nova Scotia, as a machine-gunner with the American Battalion of the Canadian Expeditionary Forces, Faust met among his fellow troopers, Tracy Richardson, the soldier of fortune in several banana republic rebellions. Unlike Richardson, though, Faust could not bear the waiting to go to war and deserted, bumming his way across Nova Scotia, through New Brunswick into Maine and on to New York. There he tried to enlist in the British Army but was rejected after failing to pass his physical examination. He was also refused by the Volunteer Ambulance Service.

By 1917, Faust had married and had begun his writing career in earnest with a number of poems and stories in such magazines as *Century, All-Story Weekly* and *Argosy*. Still determined to get into the war, he managed to join the U.S. Army Engineers. Ironically, for all his effort, he developed flu in training which led to a life-long heart ailment. His World War I career was a complete washout and it nagged him almost as much as his failure to graduate from UC.

The great Munsey editor Bob Davis is credited with giving Faust his first real impetus as a writer. In 1918, Davis is said to have presented Faust a copy of Zane Grey's *Riders of the Purple Sage* (1912). Faust read it and was much impressed. Soon after, he wrote a novel himself and called it *The Untamed*. It was published in Munsey's *All-Story Weekly* on December 7, 1918, under the name Max Brand.

The famous two-syllable pen-name was the idea of Sophie Treadwell, the wife of a sports writer for the New York *Herald-Tribune* who was a friend of Faust's. Mrs. Treadwell maintained that the ideal name—one easily remembered—should contain two monosyllables, with the same vowel sound in each. It was an exceptional piece of advice and, following her own prescription, she came up with the name Max Brand. Faust happily adopted it as his own.

Whistling Dan Berry, the "Untamed" of the novel, was one of the most popular of all the hundreds of Brand heroes and the novel was among the top five or six he would write. There was a touch of the poet in the prose of *The Untamed*. One of its most quoted passages is the closing paragraph of the novel, more than a little indebted to the close of Jack London's *The Call of the Wild*.

> Far off, above the rushing of the wind, he heard the weird whistling, a thrilling and unearthly music. It was sad with the beauty of the night. It was joyous with the exultation of the wind. It might have been the voice of some god who rode the northern storm south, south after the wild geese, south with the untamed.

Faust killed off Dan Berry in a sequel to *The Untamed, The Seventh Man,* which appeared in *Argosy-All Story Weekly* in

1921. The act so outraged his readers that Faust's editor wheedled a fourth and final novel, *Dan Berry's Daughter* (1923) from the author, but nothing could induce him to bring Dan back to life as Conan Doyle had resurrected Sherlock Holmes after a similar public outcry a quarter-century earlier.

The Untamed has sold about 1,000,000 copies since it was published and has twice been the subject of a Hollywood film, the first version starring Tom Mix in 1920.

Nine years after his first published story, Faust was making four cents a word in the pulps (the highest paid pulp writer of his time) and the literary agent Carl Brandt estimated that his number one client was writing between 1,750,000 and 2 million words a year. Faust's markets included the full range of the pulps as well as the important "slick" magazines of the period: *Harper's, American, Collier's Esquire, Liberty* and *Saturday Evening Post.*

In 1926, Faust moved to Italy and bought the 22-room Villa Negli Ulivi. With upwards of 10 servants running the household, Faust's friends said the writer became "a modern Lorenzo...a man who lived like a Renaissance prince." He grew to love Italy second only to his own country and, strange to record, wrote some of his best western fiction while living under the Florentine sun, near writers like D. H. Lawrence and Aldous Huxley.

Italy provided Faust endless inspiration for his verse, too, and while he churned out his fiction stories with never a look backward (and never a revision), he worked like a lapidary on his poetry. In such a moment of creative ecstasy Faust wrote his daughter: "I plan a new poem, a direct return to the interests of my boyhood. I sit down one morning and begin to write. I get out 19 lines absolutely different from anything I've ever done before...It seems that I have touched an electric core of existence. Even God cannot feel more happiness than comes to me at times."

This joyous paragraph on 19 lines of poetry came from the same man who was writing two million words of fiction a year. Faust's close friend Leonard Bacon, in the *Saturday Review of Literature* in 1944, wrote "With a capacity for friendship that went beyond imagination, Frederick Faust was to me poetry incarnate. He lived, moved and had his being in, for, and because of it. His legions of romance were written so that he might have leisure to seek poetry and pursue it." Another friend said Faust exhausted himself over his poems, treating each as a sculptor treats his block of rough-hewn stone as it begins to take shape, seldom satisfied with the progress or the result. Bacon says Faust once threw in the fireplace a 10,000-line epic poem because he was disappointed in the way it turned out.

By the 1930's, Frederick Faust was one of the highest paid writers of the world. His exact earnings are not known, but in this peak period it is likely that his writing income exceeded $100,000 a year. As an example of this incredible fiction factory's income, the Street and Smith magazine *Western Story* paid Faust five cents a word for his fiction and bought a total of 307 stories from him in all, probably an all-time record. Faust, more than once, made $75,000 a year from this magazine alone.

Time Magazine was awed by Faust's expenditures and remarked on his "squads of servants, instructors and tutors for his children" and Faust himself wrote dejectedly to his daughter, ". . . always there is an increasing demand for money. I need to make seventy thousand dollars a year simply to keep my mouth and nose above water."

Faust's most famous western novel, *Destry Rides Again*, appeared in *Western Story* in 1930. Only Zane Grey's *Nevada* and Jack Schaefer's *Shane* are believed to have sold more copies than *Destry* which has exhausted at least 15 editions so far. Three film versions of the Faust novel have been made, starring Tom Mix in 1932, James Stewart (and Marlene Dietrich) in 1939, and Audie Murphy in 1954.

In 1935, the name Kildare replaced Destry in the Faust pantheon of money-makers. Faust had used the name in a 1926 pirate story (it is also a county in Ireland and the name of a favorite horse of King Edward VII of England), but the name didn't become a part of the American language until it was coupled with the title "Dr." In the March, 1936, *Cosmopolitan*, appeared the Max Brand story "Interns Can't Take Money" which was the first nugget of the Kildare gold mine. The young doctor was based on Faust's friend from his Berkeley days, George Winthrop "Dixie" Fish.

In 1938, Faust tapped his highest-paying writing market—Hollywood—and if everything about his career seems cloaked in a bigger-than-life legend, his Hollywood days only added to it. In two years of work for Metro-Goldwyn-Mayer Studios, for example, he wrote the original stories for seven Dr. Kildare movies. The first film of the series was ready for shooting in 13 days. (The first screen Kildare was not, as most people think, Lew Ayres, but an upcoming actor named Joel McCrea. Ayres made the role famous, however, as Lionel Barrymore made the character Dr. Leonard Gillespie famous. On the television series, actors Richard Chamberlain in the title role and Raymond Massey as Gillespie breathed life into the characters for a new generation.)

Faust also worked for Columbia, RKO and Warner Brothers Studios and was earning $3,000 a week with the latter when, at the age of 51, he quit to go off to war.

His astounding record in Hollywood can probably never be surpassed. Over 70 films have been made from Faust's books, stories and screenplays. In one period alone, 1921-22, seven major films were released in the 12-month period, all of which were based on Faust's works. In his last days at Warner Brothers, Faust developed a system both in his writing and in his drinking. Frank Gruber, who knew "Heinie" Faust in this period, says Faust wrote only in the morning, coming to work at nine-thirty and turning out exactly 14 pages of script—no more no less—seated on a sofa, his typewriter on a straight-backed chair before him. A quart thermos of whiskey he brought with him for the session and it disappeared before noon. His lunch, Gruber said, consisted of a dozen or more drinks. The day's total of alcohol: close to two quarts.

"He was the most prolific writer of all time," Gruber said, adding, "He was also the biggest boozer I have ever known."

In any discussion of Faust's life and career there is a danger of becoming overwhelmed by his gigantic capacity for work. The facts of his writing career are so fantastic, one becomes hypnotized by the sheer improbability of the statistics. Faust himself wrote to a friend in 1934 a letter that touched on his gargantuan output: "In the summer of 1920," he wrote, "in one period I wrote in 13 days a serial, two long novelettes and 190,000 words. . . Altogether I've written between 24 and 25 million words during 17 years or the equivalent, at 70,000 words a book, of some 350 novels. These are rather startling facts, but I want to call your attention to the undoubted truth that one fairly good novel would outweigh all the mass of material I have written."

It has been said that Edgar Wallace, J. S. Fletcher and E. Phillips Oppenheim, three of America's most prolific writers (with a combined total of 105 years of productivity) could not equal Faust's superhuman output.

His books sold an average of 20,000 copies each and have been published in over ten countries (not counting pirated editions in Japan, Holland and the Balkans). In 1926, ten of Faust's novels

Frederick Schiller Faust—"Max Brand" (Author's files)

appeared under five pen-names. In 1927, he published nine books under four names and, in 1928, seven books under three names. And so it went.

Nothing can overshadow such an unparalleled bulk of work—some 628 separate items in all, including 196 novels of 50,000 words or more, 226 novelettes, 162 short stories and 44 poems.

Still, underneath this mountain of paper and string of statistics, there was a very likeable man. Brandt and other close friends called him "Heinie" and recalled him as a six-foot-two-inch, magnetically handsome man with a deep, resonant voice that captivated those who listened to him read poetry. He was a highly cultured man who loved good music (Bach in particular), good food and drink. The latter indulgence ranged from rare vintage wines to corn whiskey.

All Faust's friends were of a single voice in recalling his great generosity and capacity for friendship and his great appetite for life and work. He developed a heart fibrillation during World War I but defied his doctors by playing vigorous rounds of golf and tennis. (Still, he had a stethoscope by his bedside and took digitalis in his orange juice.)

Of his energy, *Time* wrote, "He could lock himself in a hotel room with two typewriters and a bottle of Irish whiskey and emerge four days later with a neatly typed, complete magazine serial." Four days, of course, was far too long.

His eccentricities were few: He disliked for his children to read his stories, preferring that they devote their time to more "worthwhile" literature; he did not keep a collection of his own books, let alone his magazine work, and Carl Brandt said that Faust would not even sign his own contracts and never wanted to see copies of his books or stories. If someone mentioned to him a particular story they especially liked, he would be polite but puzzled. He could seldom recall a specific story he had written and had no desire to recall them once they were published.

Frederick Faust died on May 11, 1944, killed in action in Italy seventeen days before his 52nd birthday, while serving as war correspondent for *Harper's*. It was less than a month before D-Day and less than two weeks before the Allied offensive at Anzio. During an assault of the 5th Army, under the command of Lt. General Mark Clark, near the hillside village of Santa Maria Infante, Faust was struck in the chest by a shell fragment. At first it was thought he was only wounded. He told litter-bearers, motioning toward other wounded soldiers, "They're worse off than I am. I feel pretty good." But he died soon afterward and was buried in a divisional cemetery at Carano and later reinterred in the Nettuno-Anzio American Cemetery.

Lt. Herbert Wadopian of Asheville, N.C., was platoon leader of the group to which Faust was attached in Italy and wrote this:

> Frederick Faust was without question the most courageous, the most likeable and the most admirable person I ever met...His courage was greater than any of his wild west characters and he went off to his death like a soldier but armed only with a walking stick. Just before the attack in which he was killed was launched, I begged him to carry at least a pistol. It was a night attack and his war correspondent's patch would provide him with no immunity at all. But he insisted on playing the game by the rules (Geneva Convention forbids the carrying of even a pocket-knife by non-combatants), so he carried a walking stick cut from an olive tree which he promised to use on any German who came close enough...

After so remarkable a career, any question of Faust's place in American literature is purely academic. For some, he has no place at all except as a sort of curiosity such as Zane Grey, James Oliver Curwood, Edgar Rice Burroughs and others. One authority on the subject of western fiction, S. Allen McElfresh, includes Faust's name in a list that includes Owen Wister, Zane Grey, Clarence E. Mulford, William McLeod Raine, Eugene Manlove Rhodes, W. C. Tuttle, Will Henry, Walter Noble Burns, James B. Hendryx, Ross Santee, Walt Coburn and Emerson Hough. It is good company, even for a poet.

His popularity an unassailable fact, most experts say that Faust's American West is a West that never was, filled with super-human men and heroic beasts, chockablock with flaming sixguns and episodes of good versus evil in which the good always reigns triumphant. Still, in the greatest measure, the decision of Faust's place in literature must be left to the audience. Over 20 million Max Brand books have been sold in the U.S. alone in the past quarter-century and the end is nowhere in sight.

A few years ago, for example, Dodd, Mead—Faust's publisher since 1927—issued the 200th and 201st books of fiction by Faust: *Wild Freedom* and *Max Brand's Best Western Stories,* edited by Faust authority William Nolan.

And, helping secure his place in American Western fiction, the

Faust story, "Wine of the Desert" (originally published in *This Week* in June 1936), is included in the prestigious collection, *The American West in Fiction*, edited by Jon Tuska (Mentor Books, 1982). There Faust resides with Mark Twain, Bret Harte, Owen Wister, Willa Cather, Ernest Haycox, Will Henry and Louis L'Amour, among other immortals of the Western genre.

That Faust was as inimitable a real-life figure as his Whistling Dan Berry or Montana Kid were in fiction, there can be little doubt. He was a frustrated poet working like a gem-cutter on a line or a word while spewing reams of publishable fiction in the direction of his agent and thence to the magazines and book publishers.

It was a significant tribute to Faust that when he died on the Italian battlefield in 1944, someone recalled and resurrected a poem he had published in *Harper's* some ten years earlier:

Only the young fear death.
A god has crossed their path, and they are sure
Of happiness, if it would but endure.
Only the young fear death;
For when companions vanish on the way
And leave us one by one
Is it not better done
Than to come lonely to the end of the day?
Only the young fear death.
The aged speak not of it. At the door
They stand with cheerful faces to the last,
Like men who on the homeward way have passed
The steps of darkness many times before.

It is a perfect epitaph for a poet.

Sources:

- Robert Easton, *Max Brand: The Big 'Westerner'* (1970).
- William F. Nolan, "Max Brand," Los Angeles *Times,* May 6, 1979.
- William F. Nolan, "The Phenomenon of Max Brand," *The Roundup*, July 1976.
- Darrell Richardson, *Max Brand: The Man and His Work* (1952).

Index

M

N

O

P

R

S

T

U

V

W

Y

Z

The way it really was, by a Southwestern historian-journalist—Esteban's life among the Zuni, Pancho Villa's raid north of the border, Mark Twain's drug scheme, the strange death of Ambrose Bierce, etc.

Southwest Saga
by William C. McGaw
(ISBN 0-914846-35-3)
160 pages. . . $5.00

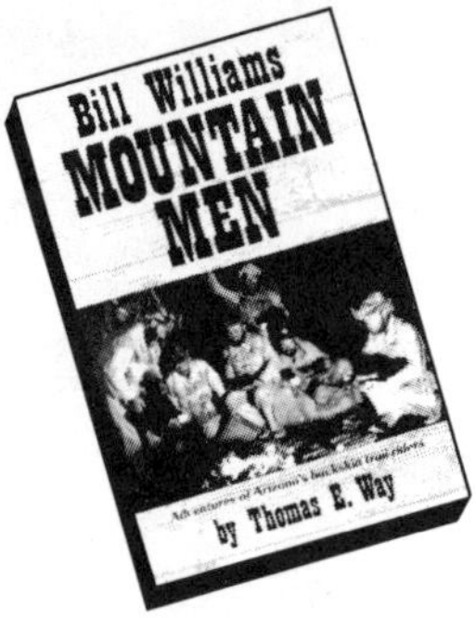

Ride the back trails with modern-day mountain men, as they preserve the memory of Arizona's rugged adventures of the past. Buckskin-clad, the mountain men stage annual treks from Williams, AZ all the way to Phoenix, AZ and to other destinations. Hilarious anecdotes.

Bill Williams Mountain Men
by Thomas E. Way
(ISBN 0-914846-30-2)
128 pages. . . $5.00

A cartoon excursion through the whimsical west of renowned cowboy cartoonist-sculptor Jim Willoughby. Western humor at its ribald best!

Cowboy Country Cartoons
by Jim Willoughby
(ISBN 0-914846-37-X)
128 pages. . . $4.50

The American cowboy had a way with words! Lingo of the American West. 2000 phrases and expressions—colorful, humorous, earthy, raunchy! Includes horse and cattle terms, rodeo talk, barb wire names, cattle brands.

Cowboy Slang
by "Frosty" Potter
(ISBN 0-914846-23-X)
128 pages. . . $5.00